THE
BIBLE
PROMISE
BOOK®

for
Difficult Times

© 2016 by Barbour Publishing, Inc.

Compiled by Linda Hang

Print ISBN 978-1-63409-683-6

eBook Editions:
Adobe Digital Edition (.epub) 978-1-63409-685-0
Kindle and MobiPocket Edition (.prc) 978-1-63409-684-3

Published by Barbour Books, an imprint of Barbour Publishing, Inc., P.O. Box 719, Uhrichsville, Ohio 44683, www.barbourbooks.com

Our mission is to publish and distribute inspirational products offering exceptional value and biblical encouragement to the masses.

Member of the
Evangelical Christian
Publishers Association

Printed in the United States of America.

THE
BIBLE
PROMISE
BOOK®
for
Difficult Times

BARBOUR BOOKS
An Imprint of Barbour Publishing, Inc.

CONTENTS

INTRODUCTION

Give all your worries to Him because He cares for you.
1 PETER 5:7 NLV

What burdens are you carrying today? Do you face a circumstance that clouds your mind and heart? We all go through these times. In fact, Jesus tells us that we will have troubles, but be encouraged! He has overcome the world (John 16:33).

The Bible is overflowing with such promises—many that speak to specific trials that we all face. Within these pages, you'll find hundreds of these heaven-sent assurances, organized by category so that you can find the encouragement you need (or to give to someone else) today.

Hold tight to these promises, and feel the arms of your heavenly Father uphold you during these difficult times. He will see you through to an even more abundant life!

ABUSE

Abuse is a topic that's hard to talk about openly. Whether it's something that lies long ago in our past, or something we are dealing with in the present, the shame that often goes along with abuse is hard to face.

But God wants to take away that sense of shame. Abuse tells lies. It says that the abused person is unworthy of love and dignity and respect. God longs to smash those lies with the love and truth of Christ's Gospel.

He is waiting to help us walk away from abuse—into a new life.

Drive out a scoffer, and strife will go out,
and quarreling and abuse will cease.
PROVERBS 22:10 ESV

The LORD is a God who avenges.
O God who avenges, shine forth.
PSALM 94:1 NIV

9

"Bless those who curse you,
pray for those who abuse you."
LUKE 6:28 ESV

He saves me from those who hate me.
Yes, You lift me above those who rise up against me.
You save me from those who want to hurt me.
PSALM 18:48 NLV

For he has not despised or scorned the suffering
of the afflicted one; he has not hidden his face
from him but has listened to his cry for help.
PSALM 22:24 NIV

Repay no one evil for evil. Have regard for good
things in the sight of all men. If it is possible, as
much as depends on you, live peaceably with all
men. Beloved, do not avenge yourselves, but rather
give place to wrath; for it is written, "Vengeance is
Mine, I will repay," says the Lord. . . . Do not be
overcome by evil, but overcome evil with good.
ROMANS 12:17–19, 21 NKJV

"Their anger will be punished, for it is bad. Their bad temper will be punished, for it is bad. I will divide them in Jacob and spread them apart in Israel."

Genesis 49:7 nlv

"If you hurt my daughters, or if you take wives other than my daughters, no man may see it. But God sees what happens between you and me."

Genesis 31:50 nlv

But you, God, see the trouble of the afflicted; you consider their grief and take it in hand. The victims commit themselves to you; you are the helper of the fatherless. Break the arm of the wicked man; call the evildoer to account for his wickedness that would not otherwise be found out.

Psalm 10:14–15 niv

He shall redeem their soul from deceit and violence: and precious shall their blood be in his sight.

Psalm 72:14 kjv

The LORD is good, a refuge in times of trouble.
He cares for those who trust in him.
NAHUM 1:7 NIV

Those who sow with tears
will reap with songs of joy.
PSALM 126:5 NIV

The Spirit himself testifies with our spirit that we
are God's children. Now if we are children, then we
are heirs—heirs of God and co-heirs with Christ,
if indeed we share in his sufferings in order that
we may also share in his glory.
ROMANS 8:16–17 NIV

Record my misery; list my tears on your scroll—
are they not in your record? Then my enemies will
turn back when I call for help. By this I will know
that God is for me. In God, whose word I praise,
in the LORD, whose word I praise—in God I trust
and am not afraid. What can man do to me?
PSALM 56:8–11 NIV

Therefore, if anyone is in Christ, the new creation
has come: The old has gone, the new is here!
2 CORINTHIANS 5:17 NIV

Strengthen the hands which hang down,
and the feeble knees.
HEBREWS 12:12 NKJV

And the afflicted people thou wilt save:
but thine eyes are upon the haughty,
that thou mayest bring them down.
2 SAMUEL 22:28 KJV

The LORD also will be a refuge for the oppressed,
a refuge in times of trouble.
PSALM 9:9 NKJV

"Broken bone for broken bone, eye for eye, tooth for
tooth. Just as he has hurt a man, so he will be hurt."
LEVITICUS 24:20 NLV

Pleasing words are like honey. They are
sweet to the soul and healing to the bones.
PROVERBS 16:24 NLV

✺

Jesus, I know You came to heal the brokenhearted.
Heal my broken heart, I pray. You came to deliver
captives into freedom. Set me free from abuse.
You came to heal those who are bruised. I ask that
You heal the scars of abuse in my heart, in my mind
and memories, and in my life. Please rescue me!

ACCIDENTS

When an accident happens, we're suddenly struck with how fragile our lives are. Our sense of safety and security shatters. Life feels shaky, as though unexpected danger lurks around every corner. It's hard to regain a sense of peace.

But the same divine energy that made the world is still at work in each and every event of our lives. What seems like catastrophe will be swept up by God's power and made into something that will bless us and those we love.

True faith means we trust God to use even the bad things for our good and His glory.

And we know that in all things God works for the good of those who love him, who have been called according to his purpose.
ROMANS 8:28 NIV

He shall cover thee with his feathers, and under his wings shalt thou trust: his truth shall be thy shield and buckler.
PSALM 91:4 KJV

*God is our refuge and strength, a very present help
in trouble. Therefore we will not fear though the
earth gives way, though the mountains be moved
into the heart of the sea, though its waters roar and
foam, though the mountains tremble at its swelling.*
PSALM 46:1–3 ESV

*The LORD shall preserve thee from all evil: he shall
preserve thy soul. The LORD shall preserve thy
going out and thy coming in from this time forth,
and even for evermore.*
PSALM 121:7–8 KJV

*Of Benjamin he said: "The beloved of the LORD shall
dwell in safety by Him, who shelters him all the day
long; and he shall dwell between His shoulders."*
DEUTERONOMY 33:12 NKJV

*You are my strength, I watch for you; you, God,
are my fortress, my God on whom I can rely.
God will go before me.*
PSALM 59:9–10 NIV

I have been in danger from rivers, in danger from bandits, in danger from my fellow Jews, in danger from Gentiles; in danger in the city, in danger in the country, in danger at sea. . . . Three times I pleaded with the Lord to take [the thorn in my flesh] away from me. But he said to me, "My grace is sufficient for you."

2 Corinthians 11:26; 12:8–9 niv

You who fear the Lord, trust in the Lord! He is their help and their shield.

Psalm 115:11 esv

Only God can say what is right or wrong. . . . He can save or put to death. . . . Listen! You who say, "Today or tomorrow we will go to this city and stay a year and make money." You do not know about tomorrow. What is your life? It is like fog. You see it and soon it is gone. What you should say is, "If the Lord wants us to, we will live and do this or that."

James 4:12–15 nlv

"Blessed are the poor in spirit, for theirs is the kingdom of heaven."

Matthew 5:3 niv

Who shall separate us from the love of Christ?
Shall trouble or hardship or persecution or
famine or nakedness or danger or sword?
Romans 8:35 niv

"The Lord himself goes before you and will be
with you; he will never leave you nor forsake you."
Deuteronomy 31:8 niv

"For I know the plans I have for you," says the
Lord, "plans for well-being and not for trouble,
to give you a future and a hope."
Jeremiah 29:11 nlv

Though I walk in the midst of trouble, You will
revive me. . .Your right hand will save me.
Psalm 138:7 nkjv

"When the earth totters, and all its inhabitants,
it is I who keep steady its pillars."
PSALM 75:3 ESV

We do not look at the things that can be seen.
We look at the things that cannot be seen.
The things that can be seen will come to an end.
But the things that cannot be seen will last forever.
2 CORINTHIANS 4:18 NLV

Be thou my strong habitation, whereunto I may
continually resort: thou hast given commandment
to save me; for thou art my rock and my fortress.
PSALM 71:3 KJV

He who lives in the safe place of the Most High will
be in the shadow of the All-powerful. I will say to the
Lord, "You are my safe and strong place, my God."
PSALM 91:1–2 NLV

God, my world seems upside down.
And yet I trust You.
The timing couldn't be worse.
And yet I trust You.
I am overwhelmed with emotion and
weariness as I try to deal with these events.
And yet I trust You.

ADDICTION

Addiction is a form of slavery. It makes us need some substance or activity to get through life. We may not realize how big the problem is, but sooner or later, we wake up to the fact that addiction has become the master. No matter what we believe intellectually about God, addiction becomes our real god. We no longer rely on the Creator of the universe for help with life's challenges. Instead, we cannot face stress or sorrow, weariness or anger, without turning to our addiction.

But God wants to set us free. Jesus came to break the bonds of slavery—including the slavery of addiction!

It is for freedom that Christ has set us free.
Stand firm, then, and do not let yourselves
be burdened again by a yoke of slavery.
GALATIANS 5:1 NIV

For I know that in me (that is, in my flesh) nothing good dwells; for to will is present with me, but how to perform what is good I do not find. For the good that I will to do, I do not do; but the evil I will not to do, that I practice. Now if I do what I will not to do, it is no longer I who do it, but sin that dwells in me. . . . O wretched man that I am! Who will deliver me from this body of death? I thank God—through Jesus Christ our Lord!

ROMANS 7:18–20, 24–25 NKJV

Peter said to them, "Be sorry for your sins and turn from them and be baptized in the name of Jesus Christ, and your sins will be forgiven. You will receive the gift of the Holy Spirit."

ACTS 2:38 NLV

The Spirit of the Lord GOD is upon me, because the LORD has anointed me to bring good news to the poor; he has sent me to bind up the brokenhearted, to proclaim liberty to the captives, and the opening of the prison to those who are bound.

ISAIAH 61:1 ESV

*I can do all this through
him who gives me strength.*
PHILIPPIANS 4:13 NIV

*God is faithful. He will not allow you to be
tempted more than you can take. But when
you are tempted, He will make a way for you.*
1 CORINTHIANS 10:13 NLV

*The creation itself will be set free from its
bondage to corruption and obtain the
freedom of the glory of the children of God.*
ROMANS 8:21 ESV

*Be sober-minded; be watchful. Your adversary the
devil prowls around like a roaring lion, seeking
someone to devour. Resist him, firm in your faith,
knowing that the same kinds of suffering are being
experienced by your brotherhood throughout the
world. And after you have suffered a little while,
the God of all grace, who has called you to his
eternal glory in Christ, will himself restore,
confirm, strengthen, and establish you.*
1 PETER 5:8–10 ESV

*Thanks be to God, who delivers
me through Jesus Christ our Lord!*
ROMANS 7:25 NIV

*So then, Christian brothers, we are not to do
what our sinful old selves want us to do. If you
do what your sinful old selves want you to do,
you will die in sin. But if, through the power of
the Holy Spirit, you destroy those actions to which
the body can be led, you will have life. All those
who are led by the Holy Spirit are sons of God.*
ROMANS 8:12–14 NLV

*Get your minds ready for good use. Keep awake.
Set your hope now and forever on the loving-favor
to be given you when Jesus Christ comes again.*
1 PETER 1:13 NLV

*Confess your faults one to another, and pray one
for another, that ye may be healed. The effectual
fervent prayer of a righteous man availeth much.*
JAMES 5:16 KJV

God bought you with a great price. So honor
God with your body. You belong to Him.
1 Corinthians 6:20 nlv

I say then: Walk in the Spirit, and you
shall not fulfill the lust of the flesh.
Galatians 5:16 nkjv

For if a man belongs to Christ, he is a new person.
The old life is gone. New life has begun.
2 Corinthians 5:17 nlv

"Therefore if the Son makes you free,
you shall be free indeed."
John 8:36 nkjv

But may all who seek you rejoice and be
glad in you; may those who long for your
saving help always say, "The Lord is great!"
Psalm 40:16 niv

25

Lord, You know I want to change. And yet again and again, I fall back into the same addictive behaviors. I get so discouraged with myself. Thank You, Lord, that You are never discouraged with me. You are always waiting to give me one more chance.

ADULTERY

We all know the technical definition of adultery, but Jesus pointed out that it's not quite that simple. The oldest meanings of the word are "to spoil, to break, to destroy." So anytime we let something break our marriage vows, destroy our relationship with our spouse, or spoil the intimacy we share, we have opened the door to adultery. Jesus said that even something as seemingly harmless as ogling someone other than our partner could damage our marriage! God asks us to protect married love, to set a shelter around it that keeps out anything that could threaten it.

" 'For this reason a man will leave his father and mother and be united to his wife, and the two will become one flesh.' So they are no longer two, but one flesh. Therefore what God has joined together, let no one separate."
MATTHEW 19:5–6 NIV

Now a Levite who lived in a remote area in the hill country of Ephraim took a concubine from Bethlehem in Judah. But she was unfaithful to him. . . . After she had been [gone] four months, her husband went to her to persuade her to return.
JUDGES 19:1–3 NIV

After a while his master's wife took notice of Joseph and said, "Come to bed with me!" But he refused. . . . And though she spoke to Joseph day after day, he refused to go to bed with her or even be with her.
GENESIS 39:7–8, 10 NIV

Then David said to Nathan, "I have sinned against the Lord." And Nathan said to him, "The Lord has taken away your sin."
2 SAMUEL 12:13 NLV

Have mercy on me, O God, according to your steadfast love; according to your abundant mercy blot out my transgressions. Wash me thoroughly from my iniquity, and cleanse me from my sin!
PSALM 51:1–2 ESV

No temptation has overtaken you that is not common to man. God is faithful, and he will not let you be tempted beyond your ability, but with the temptation he will also provide the way of escape, that you may be able to endure it.
1 CORINTHIANS 10:13 ESV

Return to the Lord your God, O Israel, for you have fallen because of your sin. Take words with you and return to the Lord. Say to Him, "Take away all sin, and receive us in kindness, that we may praise You with our lips."
HOSEA 14:1–2 NLV

The teachers of the law and the Pharisees brought in a woman caught in adultery. . . . [Jesus] said to them, "Let any one of you who is without sin be the first to throw a stone at her." . . . Jesus straightened up and asked her, "Woman, where are they? Has no one condemned you?" "No one, sir," she said. "Then neither do I condemn you," Jesus declared. "Go now and leave your life of sin."
JOHN 8:3, 7, 10–11 NIV

You understand us, Lord. You know what we are facing. You have a plan for us. Your Spirit longs to lead us forward into a future of hope and love and strength. We trust in You.

ALCOHOL ABUSE

When we abuse alcohol, our relationships suffer. Our physical health suffers. We have less energy for the people and activities we care about most. And most of all, our relationship with God suffers.

God wants us at our best, emotionally, physically, intellectually, socially. Alcohol abuse gets in the way of this. It's not that God is a goody-goody teetotaler! But our deepest connections with Him can thrive only when we are becoming the people He created us to be. He doesn't want anything to hinder that—including alcohol.

But the fruit that comes from having the Holy Spirit in our lives is. . .being the boss over our own desires. . . . If the Holy Spirit is living in us, let us be led by Him in all things.
GALATIANS 5:22–23, 25 NLV

Do not get drunk on wine, which leads to debauchery. Instead, be filled with the Spirit.
EPHESIANS 5:18 NIV

Happy are you, O land, when your king is the son of the nobility, and your princes feast at the proper time, for strength, and not for drunkenness!
ECCLESIASTES 10:17 ESV

"Be careful, or your hearts will be weighed down with carousing, drunkenness and the anxieties of life, and that day will close on you suddenly like a trap."
LUKE 21:34 NIV

Therefore, with minds that are alert and fully sober, set your hope on the grace to be brought to you when Jesus Christ is revealed at his coming.
1 PETER 1:13 NIV

Wake up from your drunken stupor,
as is right, and do not go on sinning.
1 CORINTHIANS 15:34 ESV

Since Christ suffered for us in the flesh, arm
yourselves also with the same mind, for he who
has suffered in the flesh has ceased from sin, that
he no longer should live the rest of his time in the
flesh for the lusts of men, but for the will of God.
For we have spent enough of our past lifetime in
doing the will of the Gentiles—when we walked
in. . .drunkenness, revelries, drinking parties.
1 PETER 4:1–3 NKJV

No temptation has overtaken you except such as is
common to man; but God is faithful, who will not
allow you to be tempted beyond what you are able,
but with the temptation will also make the way of
escape, that you may be able to bear it.
1 CORINTHIANS 10:13 NKJV

33

*I know You are helping me, Jesus. I believe
You are with me. Please send human helpers, too.
Give me the courage to let others know I have this
problem—and then to ask for their help. Help me
to focus outward, on others, rather than on my own
situation. Give me a strong network to depend
on so that I can learn new ways to live.*

ANGER

The Bible tells us not to nurse our anger. Instead of dwelling on it, the psalmist says we should turn away from it. Instead of feeding it until we explode, we are to let it go. There's nothing wrong with feeling angry sometimes—but when we let our anger drive us, when we lose control of ourselves because we're so full of rage, then we're likely to hurt those around us.

Acknowledge your angry feelings. But then give them to God. Allow Him to be the container that holds your temper—and keeps it from hurting others.

Stop being angry. Turn away from fighting. Do not trouble yourself. It leads only to wrong-doing.
PSALM 37:8 NLV

Do not make friends with a hot-tempered person, do not associate with one easily angered.
PROVERBS 22:24 NIV

Men who speak against others set a city on fire,
but wise men turn away anger.
PROVERBS 29:8 NLV

If you are angry, do not let it become sin.
Get over your anger before the day is finished.
EPHESIANS 4:26 NLV

A hot-tempered person stirs up conflict,
but the one who is patient calms a quarrel.
PROVERBS 15:18 NIV

Whoever is slow to anger is better than the mighty,
and he who rules his spirit than he who takes a city.
PROVERBS 16:32 ESV

Good sense makes one slow to anger,
and it is his glory to overlook an offense.
PROVERBS 19:11 ESV

Wherefore, my beloved brethren, let every man
be swift to hear, slow to speak, slow to wrath.
JAMES 1:19 KJV

A hot-tempered person must pay the penalty;
rescue them, and you will have to do it again.
PROVERBS 19:19 NIV

Like a city whose walls are broken through
is a person who lacks self-control.
PROVERBS 25:28 NIV

The vexation of a fool is known at once,
but the prudent ignores an insult.
PROVERBS 12:16 ESV

Fathers, do not provoke your children,
lest they become discouraged.
COLOSSIANS 3:21 NKJV

A stone is heavy, and the sand weighty;
but a fool's wrath is heavier than them both.
Wrath is cruel, and anger is outrageous;
but who is able to stand before envy?
PROVERBS 27:3–4 KJV

Put out of your life all these things: bad feelings about other people, anger, temper, loud talk, bad talk which hurts other people, and bad feelings which hurt other people.
EPHESIANS 4:31 NLV

The proud and arrogant person—"Mocker" is his name—behaves with insolent fury.
PROVERBS 21:24 NIV

A gentle answer turns away wrath, but a harsh word stirs up anger.
PROVERBS 15:1 NIV

If the ruler becomes angry with you, do not back away. If you are quiet, much wrong-doing may be put aside.
ECCLESIASTES 10:4 NLV

I desire therefore that the men pray everywhere, lifting up holy hands, without wrath and doubting.
1 TIMOTHY 2:8 NKJV

God, remind me that the sun should not go down on my anger. Help me not to go to bed nursing a grudge that will haunt my sleep and get up with me in the morning. Instead, let me value my relationships enough that I commit myself to working through the conflicts that arise. I know You want us to live in harmony.

ANXIETY

It's easy to be anxious. Are our loved ones safe?
Will we have enough money for what we need?
Will our friends accept us? Will we be able to
get everything done? Anxieties pile up around
us everywhere we turn.

We need to learn to transform our anxiety
into prayer. Each time we find ourselves
fretting over what will happen regarding some
situation, we can turn over that specific set of
circumstances to God. As we make this practice
a habit, we will find our trust in God growing.
Instead of anxiety, Christ will dwell at the center
of our lives.

Cast all your anxiety on him
because he cares for you.
1 PETER 5:7 NIV

Anxiety weighs down the heart,
but a kind word cheers it up.
PROVERBS 12:25 NIV

Trust in the LORD with all thine heart; and lean
not unto thine own understanding. In all thy ways
acknowledge him, and he shall direct thy paths.
PROVERBS 3:5–6 KJV

Be anxious for nothing, but in everything by prayer
and supplication, with thanksgiving, let your
requests be made known to God; and the peace of
God, which surpasses all understanding, will guard
your hearts and minds through Christ Jesus.
PHILIPPIANS 4:6–7 NKJV

My people will abide in a peaceful habitation,
in secure dwellings, and in quiet resting places.
ISAIAH 32:18 ESV

Some trust in chariots and some in horses,
but we trust in the name of the LORD our God.
PSALM 20:7 NIV

When anxiety was great within me,
your consolation brought me joy.
PSALM 94:19 NIV

"The seed that was planted among thorns is like some people who listen to the Word. But the cares of this life let thorns come up. A love for riches and always wanting other things let thorns grow. These things do not give the Word room to grow so it does not give grain."

MARK 4:18–19 NLV

The Lord says, "Stand by where the roads cross, and look. Ask for the old paths, where the good way is, and walk in it. And you will find rest for your souls.

JEREMIAH 6:16 NLV

Surely I have calmed and quieted my soul,
like a weaned child with his mother;
like a weaned child is my soul within me.

PSALM 131:2 NKJV

Trust in the LORD and do good;
dwell in the land and enjoy safe pasture.

PSALM 37:3 NIV

Trouble and anguish have found me out,
but your commandments are my delight.

PSALM 119:143 ESV

*These things I have spoken unto you, that in
me ye might have peace. In the world ye
shall have tribulation: but be of good cheer;
I have overcome the world.*
JOHN 16:33 KJV

*Unless the Lord builds the house, its builders work
for nothing. Unless the Lord watches over the city,
the men who watch over it stay awake for nothing.
You rise up early, and go to bed late, and work hard
for your food, all for nothing. For the Lord gives
to His loved ones even while they sleep.*
PSALM 127:1–2 NLV

*First of all, look for the holy nation of God.
Be right with Him. All these other
things will be given to you also.*
MATTHEW 6:33 NLV

*Better is a handful of quietness than two
hands full of toil and a striving after wind.*
ECCLESIASTES 4:6 ESV

Indeed, he who watches over Israel
will neither slumber nor sleep.
PSALM 121:4 NIV

For in Scripture it says: "See, I lay a stone in Zion,
a chosen and precious cornerstone, and the one
who trusts in him will never be put to shame."
Now to you who believe, this stone is precious.
But to those who do not believe, "The stone the
builders rejected has become the cornerstone."
1 PETER 2:6–7 NIV

The Lord is my strength and my safe cover.
My heart trusts in Him, and I am helped. So my
heart is full of joy. I will thank Him with my song.
PSALM 28:7 NLV

Wait for the LORD; be strong, and let your heart
take courage; wait for the LORD!
PSALM 27:14 ESV

But godliness with contentment is great gain.
1 TIMOTHY 6:6 KJV

"The LORD turn his face toward
you and give you peace."
NUMBERS 6:26 NIV

Then they were glad that the waters were quiet,
and he brought them to their desired haven.
PSALM 107:30 ESV

When everything is going well, I'm not too anxious,
Lord. I feel like I'm in control. My sense of security is
stable. But when I feel threatened or overwhelmed, I start
to get anxious. Use my anxiety, Lord, to remind me that
I'm dependent on Your love. Let each nagging fear be a
nudge that turns me toward You and Your strength.

45

ARGUMENTS

God doesn't want us to quarrel. He calls us instead to kindness. This may mean setting our own opinions aside as being not all that important. . .so that instead we can hear what another thinks. It may mean letting go of our own choices. . .so we can make room for another to choose. It may require that we keep our mouth shut when angry words threaten to burst out of us. . .so that someone else has a chance to speak.

Does it (whatever "it" is) really matter that much? Or can we choose to make kindness matter far more?

Don't have anything to do with foolish and stupid arguments, because you know they produce quarrels. And the Lord's servant must not be quarrelsome but must be kind to everyone, able to teach, not resentful.
2 TIMOTHY 2:23–24 NIV

What causes fights and quarrels among you? Don't they come from your desires that battle within you? You desire but do not have, so you kill. You covet but you cannot get what you want, so you quarrel and fight. . . . You adulterous people, don't you know that friendship with the world means enmity against God? . . . But he gives us more grace. That is why Scripture says: "God opposes the proud but shows favor to the humble." Submit yourselves, then, to God. Resist the devil, and he will flee from you. Come near to God and he will come near to you. Wash your hands, you sinners, and purify your hearts, you double-minded. . . . Humble yourselves before the Lord, and he will lift you up.

JAMES 4:1–2, 4, 6–8, 10 NIV

We demolish arguments and every pretension that sets itself up against the knowledge of God, and we take captive every thought to make it obedient to Christ.

2 CORINTHIANS 10:5 NIV

"Would they argue with useless words, with speeches that have no value?"

JOB 15:3 NIV

*I want you to stress these things, so that those
who have trusted in God may be careful to devote
themselves to doing what is good. These things are
excellent and profitable for everyone. But avoid
foolish controversies and genealogies and arguments
and quarrels about the law, because these are
unprofitable and useless. Warn a divisive person
once, and then warn them a second time.
After that, have nothing to do with them.*
TITUS 3:8–10 NIV

*No one wants what is right and fair in court.
And no one argues his cause with the truth.
They trust in what is false, and speak lies.
They plan to make trouble and do what is sinful.*
ISAIAH 59:4 NLV

*Put on therefore, as the elect of God, holy and
beloved, bowels of mercies, kindness, humbleness
of mind, meekness, longsuffering; forbearing one
another, and forgiving one another, if any man
have a quarrel against any: even as Christ
forgave you, so also do ye.*
COLOSSIANS 3:12 –13 KJV

An argument started among the disciples as to which of them would be the greatest. Jesus, knowing their thoughts, took a little child and had him stand beside him. Then he said to them, "Whoever welcomes this little child in my name welcomes me; and whoever welcomes me welcomes the one who sent me. For it is the one who is least among you all who is the greatest."

LUKE 9:46–48 NIV

Do all things without grumbling or disputing, that you may be blameless and innocent, children of God without blemish in the midst of a crooked and twisted generation, among whom you shine as lights in the world, holding fast to the word of life, so that in the day of Christ I may be proud that I did not run in vain or labor in vain.

PHILIPPIANS 2:14–16 ESV

I tell you this so that no one may deceive you by fine-sounding arguments. For though I am absent from you in body, I am present with you in spirit and delight to see how disciplined you are and how firm your faith in Christ is.

COLOSSIANS 2:4–5 NIV

May I use my conversations only for Your glory, Lord. Remind me to seek to bless others with each thing I say. If arguments and cross words pour out of me, how can I claim to be filled with Your Spirit? Cleanse my heart first, dear God, and then my mouth and all its words, so that my life is not filled with contradiction.

BETRAYAL

People let us down. Sometimes it's unintentional, and that hurts bad enough. It's even worse when a friend purposely stabs us in the back. The hurt can be overwhelming. It's only natural to want to put up our guard.

It's far more challenging to follow Christ's example. He, too, knew what it was like to be betrayed by a friend. And yet He never spoke sharp words, never sought to return the blow in any way.

If we are followers of Jesus Christ, then we, too, must find ways to respond with love to those who have hurt us.

And while they abode in Galilee, Jesus said unto them, The Son of man shall be betrayed into the hands of men: and they shall kill him, and the third day he shall be raised again.
MATTHEW 17:22–23 KJV

"If his sons forsake my law and do not follow my statutes, if they violate my decrees and fail to keep my commands, I will punish their sin with the rod, their iniquity with flogging; but I will not take my love from him, nor will I ever betray my faithfulness."
PSALM 89:30–33 NIV

The eyes of the LORD keep watch over knowledge, but he overthrows the words of the traitor.
PROVERBS 22:12 ESV

There are six things which the Lord hates, yes, seven that are hated by Him. . .a person who tells lies about someone else. . . . My son, keep the teaching of your father, and do not turn away from the teaching of your mother. Hold them always to your heart. Tie them around your neck. They will lead you when you walk. They will watch over you when you sleep, and they will talk with you when you wake up. For the word is a lamp. The teaching is a light.
PROVERBS 6:16, 19–23 NLV

*Know therefore that the L*ORD *your God is God,
the faithful God who keeps covenant and steadfast
love with those who love him and keep his
commandments, to a thousand generations.*

*My companion attacks his friends; he violates
his covenant. His talk is smooth as butter,
yet war is in his heart; his words are more
soothing than oil, yet they are drawn swords.
Cast your cares on the L*ORD *and he will sustain
you; he will never let the righteous be shaken.*

PSALM 55:20–22 NIV

*For I have received of the Lord that which also I
delivered unto you, that the Lord Jesus the same
night in which he was betrayed took bread: and
when he had given thanks, he brake it, and said,
Take, eat: this is my body, which is broken for you:
this do in remembrance of me.*

1 CORINTHIANS 11:23–24 KJV

Preserve me, O God, for in you I take refuge. I say to the LORD, "You are my Lord; I have no good apart from you." . . . Therefore my heart is glad, and my whole being rejoices; my flesh also dwells secure. For you will not abandon my soul.

PSALM 16:1–2, 9–10 ESV

And David went out to meet them, and answered and said unto them, If ye be come peaceably unto me to help me, mine heart shall be knit unto you: but if ye be come to betray me to mine enemies, seeing there is no wrong in mine hands, the God of our fathers look thereon, and rebuke it.

1 CHRONICLES 12:17 KJV

See that no one repays anyone evil for evil, but always seek to do good to one another and to everyone. Rejoice always, pray without ceasing, give thanks in all circumstances; for this is the will of God in Christ Jesus for you.

1 THESSALONIANS 5:15–18 ESV

"You will be betrayed even by parents, brothers and sisters, relatives and friends, and they will put some of you to death. Everyone will hate you because of me. But not a hair of your head will perish. Stand firm, and you will win life."

LUKE 21:16–19 NIV

Ah, you destroyer, who yourself have not been destroyed, you traitor, whom none has betrayed! When you have ceased to destroy, you will be destroyed; and when you have finished betraying, they will betray you. O LORD, be gracious to us; we wait for you. Be our arm every morning, our salvation in the time of trouble.

ISAIAH 33:1–2 ESV

Use my pain at this betrayal for Your purposes, Creator God. Teach me through it. Draw me closer to You. Deepen my compassion for others.

CHALLENGES

We're not likely ever to face an army of horses and chariots—but some days, the challenges in our lives can seem just as threatening as any battlefield. When that happens, we need to follow the advice given in the Bible. First, remember all that God has done for us in the past. Second, believe that He is the One who will fight our battles, not us. We can rely on Him for the victory.

The load was so heavy we did not have the strength to keep going. . . . This happened so we would not put our trust in ourselves, but in God Who raises the dead.
2 CORINTHIANS 1:8–9 NLV

"In this world you will have trouble. But take heart! I have overcome the world."
JOHN 16:33 NIV

*You need to persevere so that when you
have done the will of God, you will
receive what he has promised.*

HEBREWS 10:36 NIV

*I also persevered in the work on this wall,
and we acquired no land, and all my servants were
gathered there for the work. Moreover, there were
at my table 150 men, Jews and officials, besides those
who came to us from the nations that were around
us. Now what was prepared at my expense for
each day was one ox and six choice sheep and birds,
and every ten days all kinds of wine in abundance.
Yet for all this I did not demand the food allowance
of the governor, because the service was too heavy on
this people. Remember for my good, O my God,
all that I have done for this people.*

NEHEMIAH 5:16–19 ESV

*"Have I not commanded you? Be strong
and courageous. Do not be afraid;
do not be discouraged, for the LORD your
God will be with you wherever you go."*

JOSHUA 1:9 NIV

57

But Jesus looked at them and said to them,
"With men this is impossible, but with
God all things are possible."
MATTHEW 19:26 NKJV

"If what is bad comes upon us, fighting, hard times,
disease, or no food, we will stand in front of this
house. And we will stand before You, (for Your name
is in this house). We will cry to You in our trouble.
And You will hear and take us out of trouble."
2 CHRONICLES 20:9 NLV

By faith he left Egypt, not fearing the king's anger;
he persevered because he saw him who is invisible.
HEBREWS 11:27 NIV

Then the Lord said to Moses, "Why do you cry
to me? Tell the people of Israel to keep going.
Lift up your special stick and put out your hand
over the sea, and divide it. Then the people
of Israel will go through the sea on dry land."
EXODUS 14:15–16 NLV

*Brothers and sisters, as an example of patience
in the face of suffering, take the prophets who
spoke in the name of the Lord. As you know,
we count as blessed those who have persevered.
You have heard of Job's perseverance and have
seen what the Lord finally brought about.
The Lord is full of compassion and mercy.*
JAMES 5:10–11 NIV

*"Many people will give up and turn away at this
time. People will hand over each other. They will
hate each other. Many false religious teachers will
come. They will fool many people and will turn
them to the wrong way. Because of people breaking
the laws and sin being everywhere, the love in the
hearts of many people will become cold. But the one
who stays true to the end will be saved."*
MATTHEW 24:10–13 NLV

*"Because you have kept My command to persevere,
I also will keep you from the hour of trial which shall
come upon the whole world, to test those who dwell
on the earth. Behold, I am coming quickly! Hold fast
what you have, that no one may take your crown."*
REVELATION 3:10–11 NKJV

※

The challenge that lies ahead, Lord, is too big for me. My self-confidence fails. I can't help but compare the enormity of the challenge to my meager ability to confront it. My faith wavers. But I know that when I admit how weak I truly am, then You have the chance to reveal Your strength. The challenge that lies ahead shrinks when I compare it to the immensity of You. And I finally realize that my perception of the challenge depends on my perspective. Keep me focused on You and Your power.

Church Discord

Scripture makes it clear that God has no patience with church arguments that spill over into gossip and backstabbing, factions and plots, outright lies and ever-accelerating hostility. It's all too easy to get sucked in—to take sides, to listen to the gossip, and even to contribute to the exaggeration and complaints that thrive in a divided church.

Conflicts are bound to happen in any family, including church families. But God's Spirit always seeks to heal and restore unity. As Christ's followers, we are called to be open to the Spirit's leading us. . .to foster peace rather than strife!

I urge you, brothers and sisters, to watch out for those who cause divisions and put obstacles in your way that are contrary to the teaching you have learned. Keep away from them.
ROMANS 16:17 NIV

*For first of all, when ye come together in the church,
I hear that there be divisions among you; and I
partly believe it. . . . Wherefore, my brethren,
when ye come together to eat, tarry one for another.*
1 CORINTHIANS 11:18, 33 KJV

*Christ gave gifts to men. He gave to some the gift
to be missionaries, some to be preachers, others to
be preachers who go from town to town. He gave
others the gift to be church leaders and teachers.
These gifts help His people work well for Him.
And then the church which is the body of
Christ will be made strong.*
EPHESIANS 4:11–12 NLV

*But we are to hold to the truth with love in our
hearts. We are to grow up and be more like Christ.
He is the leader of the church. Christ has put each
part of the church in its right place. Each part helps
other parts. This is what is needed to keep the whole
body together. In this way, the whole body grows
strong in love.*
EPHESIANS 4:15–16 NLV

God has put the body together. . .so that there should be no division in the body, but that its parts should have equal concern for each other. If one part suffers, every part suffers with it; if one part is honored, every part rejoices with it. Now you are the body of Christ, and each one of you is a part of it.

1 CORINTHIANS 12:24–27 NIV

Now I beseech you, brethren, by the name of our Lord Jesus Christ, that ye all speak the same thing, and that there be no divisions among you; but that ye be perfectly joined together in the same mind and in the same judgment. For it hath been declared unto me of you, my brethren, by them which are of the house of Chloe, that there are contentions among you. Now this I say, that every one of you saith, I am of Paul; and I of Apollos; and I of Cephas; and I of Christ. Is Christ divided?

1 CORINTHIANS 1:10–13 KJV

"And I tell you, you are Peter, and on this rock I will build my church, and the gates of hell shall not prevail against it."

MATTHEW 16:18 ESV

*These are grumblers, complainers, walking according
to their own lusts; and they mouth great swelling
words, flattering people to gain advantage. But you,
beloved, remember the words which were spoken
before by the apostles of our Lord Jesus Christ:
how they told you that there would be mockers in
the last time who would walk according to their
own ungodly lusts. These are sensual persons, who
cause divisions, not having the Spirit. But you,
beloved, building yourselves up on your most holy
faith, praying in the Holy Spirit, keep yourselves
in the love of God, looking for the mercy of our
Lord Jesus Christ unto eternal life.*

JUDE 1:16–21 NKJV

*God has put all things under Christ's power and
has made Him to be the head leader over all things
of the church. The church is the body of Christ.
It is filled by Him Who fills all things everywhere
with Himself.*

EPHESIANS 1:22–23 NLV

Bless those who persecute you; bless and do not curse them. Rejoice with those who rejoice, weep with those who weep. Live in harmony with one another. Do not be haughty, but associate with the lowly. Never be wise in your own sight. Repay no one evil for evil, but give thought to do what is honorable in the sight of all. If possible, so far as it depends on you, live peaceably with all.
ROMANS 12:14–18 ESV

Dear Lord, make me a peacemaker. Give me the words to say that will build bridges between the groups and individuals embroiled in conflict.

DEATH OF A LOVED ONE

Our hearts are breaking inside us, and all the while we're forced to cope with day-to-day concerns. Emotionally, spiritually, and physically, we are in pain. Our lives will never be the same after losing a loved one.

There is no quick and easy way through this time. Grief has no shortcuts. But God has promised to be with us always. Nothing can separate us from His love—and He will walk with us, day by day and moment by moment, as we travel on grief's journey.

"Blessed are those who mourn,
for they shall be comforted."
MATTHEW 5:4 ESV

"I trust God for the same things they are looking for.
I am looking for the dead to rise."
ACTS 24:15 NLV

Weeping may endure for a night,
but joy comes in the morning.
PSALM 30:5 NKJV

"He will wipe away every tear from their eyes,
and death shall be no more, neither shall there
be mourning, nor crying, nor pain anymore,
for the former things have passed away."
REVELATION 21:4 ESV

And provide for those who grieve in Zion—
to bestow on them a crown of beauty instead of
ashes, the oil of joy instead of mourning, and a
garment of praise instead of a spirit of despair.
ISAIAH 61:3 NIV

The LORD is near to those
who have a broken heart.
PSALM 34:18 NKJV

Surely he hath borne our griefs,
and carried our sorrows.
ISAIAH 53:4 KJV

*"For sure, I tell you, you will cry and have sorrow,
but the world will have joy. You will have sorrow,
but your sorrow will turn into joy. . . . You are sad
now. I will see you again and then your hearts will
be full of joy. No one can take your joy from you."*
JOHN 16:20, 22 NLV

*Rejoice with them that do rejoice,
and weep with them that weep.*
ROMANS 12:15 KJV

*The lowly he sets on high,
and those who mourn are lifted to safety.*
JOB 5:11 NIV

*To everything there is a season, a time for
every purpose under heaven: a time to be born,
and a time to die. . .a time to weep, and a time
to laugh; a time to mourn, and a time to dance,*
ECCLESIASTES 3:1–2, 4 NKJV

*"I will heal them; I will guide them and restore
comfort to Israel's mourners, creating praise on their
lips. Peace, peace, to those far and near," says the LORD.*
ISAIAH 57:18–19 NIV

Brothers and sisters, we do not want you to be uninformed about those who sleep in death, so that you do not grieve like the rest of mankind, who have no hope. For we believe that Jesus died and rose again, and so we believe that God will bring with Jesus those who have fallen asleep in him. According to the Lord's word, we tell you that we who are still alive, who are left until the coming of the Lord, will certainly not precede those who have fallen asleep. For the Lord himself will come down from heaven, with a loud command, with the voice of the archangel and with the trumpet call of God, and the dead in Christ will rise first. After that, we who are still alive and are left will be caught up together with them in the clouds to meet the Lord in the air. And so we will be with the Lord forever. Therefore encourage one another with these words.

1 Thessalonians 4:13–18 niv

My heart was grieved and my spirit embittered. . . . Yet I am always with you; you hold me by my right hand. You guide me with your counsel, and afterward you will take me into glory.

Psalm 73:21, 23–24 niv

69

Be afflicted, and mourn, and weep: let your laughter be turned to mourning, and your joy to heaviness. Humble yourselves in the sight of the Lord, and he shall lift you up.
JAMES 4:9–10 KJV

You have turned for me my mourning into dancing; you have loosed my sackcloth and clothed me with gladness, that my glory may sing your praise and not be silent. O LORD my God, I will give thanks to you forever!
PSALM 30:11–12 ESV

I wasn't prepared for how much this would hurt, Jesus. Please walk with me through my grief. Let me allow this suffering to draw me closer to You.

DEPRESSION

Depression is more than just the daily sadnesses that come and go. It's a deep-seated feeling that grabs hold of us and doesn't let go, day after day. It can take a toll on our social lives, our professional lives, our spiritual lives, and our health.

As Christians we may feel we should be immune to depression. But depression is no sin! God has promised us He will be especially close to us when we go through these bleak times. He will be there at our side, waiting to lead us into His joy once more.

Blessed be the God and Father of our Lord Jesus Christ, the Father of mercies and God of all comfort.
2 CORINTHIANS 1:3 ESV

Shout for joy, you heavens; rejoice, you earth; burst into song, you mountains! For the LORD comforts his people and will have compassion on his afflicted ones.
ISAIAH 49:13 NIV

The LORD is close to the brokenhearted
and saves those who are crushed in spirit.
PSALM 34:18 NIV

Answer me speedily, O LORD; my spirit fails!
Do not hide Your face from me, lest I be like those
who go down into the pit. Cause me to hear Your
lovingkindness in the morning, for in You do I trust.
PSALM 143:7–8 NKJV

He heals the brokenhearted
and binds up their wounds.
PSALM 147:3 NIV

"He found him in a desert land, and in the howling
waste of the wilderness; he encircled him, he cared
for him, he kept him as the apple of his eye."
DEUTERONOMY 32:10 ESV

"Until now you have not asked for anything
in My name. Ask and you will receive.
Then your joy will be full."
JOHN 16:24 NLV

*I waited patiently for the L*ORD*; and He inclined to me, and heard my cry. He also brought me up out of a horrible pit, out of the miry clay, and set my feet upon a rock, and established my steps. He has put a new song in my mouth—praise to our God.*

PSALM 40:1–3 NKJV

Why are you cast down, O my soul? And why are you disquieted within me? Hope in God; for I shall yet praise Him, the help of my countenance and my God.

PSALM 42:11 NKJV

In the beginning was the Word, and the Word was with God, and the Word was God. He was in the beginning with God. All things were made through him, and without him was not any thing made that was made. In him was life, and the life was the light of men. The light shines in the darkness, and the darkness has not overcome it.

JOHN 1:1–5 ESV

Bear one another's burdens, and so fulfill the law of Christ.

GALATIANS 6:2 ESV

Blessed be God, even the Father of our Lord Jesus Christ, the Father of mercies, and the God of all comfort; who comforteth us in all our tribulation, that we may be able to comfort them which are in any trouble, by the comfort wherewith we ourselves are comforted of God.

2 Corinthians 1:3–4 kjv

"He reached down from on high and took hold of me; he drew me out of deep waters. He rescued me from my powerful enemy, from my foes, who were too strong for me. They confronted me in the day of my disaster, but the Lord was my support. He brought me out into a spacious place; he rescued me because he delighted in me."

2 Samuel 22:17–20 niv

But You, O Lord, are a shield for me, my glory and the One who lifts up my head.

Psalm 3:3 nkjv

"You are sad now. I will see you again and then your hearts will be full of joy. No one can take your joy from you."

John 16:22 nlv

"And you, child, will be called the prophet of the Most High; for you will go before the Lord to prepare his ways, to give knowledge of salvation to his people. . .because of the tender mercy of our God, whereby the sunrise shall visit us from on high to give light to those who sit in darkness and in the shadow of death, to guide our feet into the way of peace."

LUKE 1:76–79 ESV

I'm waiting patiently for You, Lord. I know You will lean down to me and hear my cry. You will draw me up out of this miry bog of depression where I'm stuck. You will set my feet on the rock and make my steps steady. And then You will put a new song in my mouth, a song of praise to God.

DISABILITIES

The Gospels are full of stories of Jesus healing people. We never hear of Him looking down on these people as being less important or less deserving of His time. Instead, He treated each one with respect and compassion—and then He raised them up.

As Christ's followers, we, too, are called to reach out to those with disabilities. We cannot heal their physical issues—but we can treat them with dignity and respect. We can make sure they are not overlooked or ignored. And we can work to bring them back into society, allowing them to contribute to our communities.

After you have suffered for awhile, God Himself will make you perfect. He will keep you in the right way. He will give you strength. He is the God of all loving-favor and has called you through Christ Jesus to share His shining-greatness forever.
1 PETER 5:10 NLV

*His followers asked Him, "Teacher, whose sin made
this man to be born blind? Was it the sin of this man
or the sin of his parents?" Jesus answered, "The sin of
this man or the sin of his parents did not make him
to be born blind. He was born blind so the work of
God would be seen in him. We must keep on doing
the work of Him Who sent Me while it is day.
Night is coming when no man can work. While I
am in the world, I am the Light of the world."*
JOHN 9:2–5 NLV

*And if the ear should say, "Because I am not an eye,
I do not belong to the body," it would not for that
reason stop being part of the body. If the whole body
were an eye, where would the sense of hearing be?
. . . God has placed the parts in the body, every one
of them, just as he wanted them to be.*
1 CORINTHIANS 12:16–18 NIV

*"You shall not curse the deaf or put a
stumbling block before the blind, but you
shall fear your God: I am the LORD."*
LEVITICUS 19:14 ESV

77

Then Jesus said to his host, "When you give a luncheon or dinner, do not invite your friends, your brothers or sisters, your relatives, or your rich neighbors; if you do, they may invite you back and so you will be repaid. But when you give a banquet, invite the poor, the crippled, the lame, the blind, and you will be blessed."

LUKE 14:12–14 NIV

The LORD said to him, "Who gave human beings their mouths? Who makes them deaf or mute? Who gives them sight or makes them blind? Is it not I, the LORD?"

EXODUS 4:11 NIV

Not only so, but we also glory in our sufferings, because we know that suffering produces perseverance; perseverance, character; and character, hope. And hope does not put us to shame, because God's love has been poured out into our hearts through the Holy Spirit, who has been given to us.

ROMANS 5:3–5 NIV

But he said to me, "My grace is sufficient for you, for my power is made perfect in weakness." Therefore I will boast all the more gladly of my weaknesses, so that the power of Christ may rest upon me.

2 Corinthians 12:9 esv

For You formed my inward parts; You covered me in my mother's womb. I will praise You, for I am fearfully and wonderfully made; marvelous are Your works, and that my soul knows very well.

Psalm 139:13–14 nkjv

Jesus answered and said unto them, Go and shew John again those things which ye do hear and see: the blind receive their sight, and the lame walk, the lepers are cleansed, and the deaf hear, the dead are raised up, and the poor have the gospel preached to them.

Matthew 11:4–5 kjv

Wherefore lift up the hands which hang down, and the feeble knees; and make straight paths for your feet, lest that which is lame be turned out of the way; but let it rather be healed.

Hebrews 12:12–13 kjv

The eye cannot say to the hand, "I have no need of you," nor again the head to the feet, "I have no need of you." On the contrary, the parts of the body that seem to be weaker are indispensable, and on those parts of the body that we think less honorable we bestow the greater honor. . . . God has so composed the body, giving greater honor to the part that lacked it, that there may be no division in the body, but that the members may have the same care for one another. If one member suffers, all suffer together; if one member is honored, all rejoice together.

1 CORINTHIANS 12:21–26 ESV

For we are his workmanship, created in Christ Jesus for good works, which God prepared beforehand, that we should walk in them.

EPHESIANS 2:10 ESV

We know that God makes all things work together for the good of those who love Him and are chosen to be a part of His plan.

ROMANS 8:28 NLV

Dear Father, may I see You in each person, no matter how broken they may appear to be on the outside. May I remember that when I serve those who are disabled, I am truly serving You.

DISAPPOINTMENT

Disappointment comes in all shapes and sizes. Maybe life itself has disappointed us. Maybe someone we counted on has let us down. Or maybe we have disappointed ourselves. Our own failures and weaknesses have forced us to realize that we're not the people we dreamed of being.

But one thing is certain: No matter what else disappoints us, God never will! When everything else lets us down—when the fig tree doesn't bud, the vines have no grapes, our crops fail, and everything in our lives is empty—we can still rejoice in God our Savior.

Though the fig tree should not blossom, nor fruit be on the vines, the produce of the olive fail and the fields yield no food, the flock be cut off from the fold and there be no herd in the stalls, yet I will rejoice in the LORD; I will take joy in the God of my salvation.
HABAKKUK 3:17–18 ESV

"You will know that I am the LORD;
those who hope in me will not be disappointed."

Now to Him who is able to do exceedingly
abundantly above all that we ask or think,
according to the power that works in us,
to Him be glory in the church by Christ Jesus
to all generations, forever and ever.
EPHESIANS 3:20–21 NKJV

I have learned to be content whatever the
circumstances. I know what it is to be in need,
and I know what it is to have plenty. I have
learned the secret of being content in any and
every situation, whether well fed or hungry,
whether living in plenty or in want. I can do
all this through him who gives me strength.
PHILIPPIANS 4:11–13 NIV

Now hope does not disappoint, because the love
of God has been poured out in our hearts by
the Holy Spirit who was given to us.
ROMANS 5:5 NKJV

Now listen, you who say, "Today or tomorrow we will go to this or that city, spend a year there, carry on business and make money." Why, you do not even know what will happen tomorrow. What is your life? You are a mist that appears for a little while and then vanishes. Instead, you ought to say, "If it is the Lord's will, we will live and do this or that."
JAMES 4:13–15 NIV

The fear of the LORD leads to life;
then one rests content, untouched by trouble.
PROVERBS 19:23 NIV

But if we have food and clothing,
we will be content with that.
1 TIMOTHY 6:8 NIV

My Christian brothers, you should be happy when you have all kinds of tests. You know these prove your faith. It helps you not to give up. Learn well how to wait so you will be strong and complete and in need of nothing.
JAMES 1:2-4 NLV

*Now the Lord of All says, "Think about your
ways! You have planted much, but gather little.
You eat, but there is not enough to fill you.
You drink, but never have your fill. You put on
clothing, but no one is warm enough. You earn
money, but put it into a bag with holes." . . . And
the people honored the Lord with fear. Then Haggai
the man of God spoke for the Lord to the people,
saying, "I am with you," says the Lord.*
HAGGAI 1:5–6, 12–13 NLV

*My soul will be satisfied as with fat and rich food,
and my mouth will praise you with joyful lips.*
PSALM 63:5 ESV

*But he said to me,
"My grace is sufficient for you."*
2 CORINTHIANS 12:9 ESV

*So do not fear, for I am with you; do not be dismayed,
for I am your God. I will strengthen you and help you;
I will uphold you with my righteous right hand.*
ISAIAH 41:10 NIV

Hope deferred makes the heart sick,
but when the desire comes, it is a tree of life.
PROVERBS 13:12 NKJV

As for me, I shall behold your face in righteousness;
when I awake, I shall be satisfied with your likeness.
PSALM 17:15 ESV

Lord, when I reach the point where I have nothing
left but You, I can finally realize that You alone are
enough. All my questions won't be answered in this
life. My circumstances may not be improved. I'll have
to let go of some of the things I've set my heart on.
But none of that matters. You are the strength
of my heart and my portion forever.

DISHONESTY

As Christ's followers, we are to believe the truth, love the truth, and walk in the truth. We are to speak the truth in love. Christ came to us full of grace and truth, but He went still further than that: He told us that He *is* the Truth personified, the Truth incarnate. We are to love the truth because Jesus is the Truth. We are to stay close to it and follow after it, because that is the way we follow our Lord. If we are Christ's representatives, then those around us should know we always speak the truth.

And the Word became flesh and dwelt among us,
and we have seen his glory, glory as of the only
Son from the Father, full of grace and truth.
JOHN 1:14 ESV

The Lord hates a false weight,
but a true weight is His joy.
PROVERBS 11:1 NLV

Dishonest money dwindles away, but whoever
gathers money little by little makes it grow.
PROVERBS 13:11 NIV

As for me, You hold me up in my honesty.
And You set me beside You forever.
PSALM 41:12 NLV

Therefore, having put away falsehood,
let each one of you speak the truth with his
neighbor, for we are members one of another.
EPHESIANS 4:25 ESV

A wicked person earns deceptive wages, but the
one who sows righteousness reaps a sure reward.
PROVERBS 11:18 NIV

Therefore seeing we have this ministry, as we have
received mercy, we faint not; but have renounced the
hidden things of dishonesty, not walking in craftiness,
nor handling the word of God deceitfully; but by
manifestation of the truth commending ourselves to
every man's conscience in the sight of God.
2 CORINTHIANS 4:1–2 KJV

"Whoever can be trusted with very little can also be trusted with much, and whoever is dishonest with very little will also be dishonest with much."

LUKE 16:10 NIV

The Lord hates lying lips, but those who speak the truth are His joy.

PROVERBS 12:22 NLV

Hear this, you who trample the needy and do away with the poor of the land, saying, "When will the New Moon be over that we may sell grain, and the Sabbath be ended that we may market wheat?"— skimping on the measure, boosting the price and cheating with dishonest scales, buying the poor with silver and the needy for a pair of sandals, selling even the sweepings with the wheat. The LORD has sworn by himself, the Pride of Jacob: "I will never forget anything they have done."

AMOS 8:4–7 NIV

Be careful to do what is right in the eyes of everyone.

ROMANS 12:17 NIV

For we aim at what is honorable not only in
the Lord's sight but also in the sight of man.
2 CORINTHIANS 8:21 ESV

These are the things you shall do: Speak each man
the truth to his neighbor; give judgment in
your gates for truth, justice, and peace.
ZECHARIAH 8:16 NKJV

The lip of truth shall be established for ever:
but a lying tongue is but for a moment.
PROVERBS 12:19 KJV

"You have heard that it was said long ago,
'You must not make a promise you cannot keep.
You must carry out your promises to the Lord.'
I tell you, do not use strong words when you make
a promise. Do not promise by heaven. It is the place
where God is. Do not promise by earth. It is where
He rests His feet. . . . Do not promise by your head.
You are not able to make one hair white or black.
Let your yes be YES. Let your no be NO.
Anything more than this comes from the devil."
MATTHEW 5:33–37 NLV

Blessed are they that do his commandments,
that they may have right to the tree of life,
and may enter in through the gates into the city.
For without are dogs, and sorcerers, and
whoremongers, and murderers, and idolaters,
and whosoever loveth and maketh a lie.

REVELATION 22:14–15 KJV

Teach me thy way, O LORD; I will walk in
thy truth: unite my heart to fear thy name.

PSALM 86:11 KJV

God, I know You never lie, for You are the God of truth.
I can trust You never to be dishonest with me. You always
keep Your promises. But Your Son called Satan a "liar
and the father of liars." Remind me always that when I
speak the truth, I am speaking Your Son's language—
but when I am dishonest, when I mislead others in any
way, I am speaking the language of my enemy.

91

DISTRUST

We first learned to trust as babies cared for by loving parents. That most basic level of trust was the foundation on which all our human relationships were built.

But sometimes parents fail to teach their children how to trust. If our parents hurt us, we may not be able to trust others, including God. Or maybe a close friend or a spouse damaged our trust later in life.

God wants to heal our distrust. He knows we can never be whole until we can trust Him. We will never have intimacy—even with God— until we can learn to trust once more.

But You brought me out when I was born. You made me trust when I drank my mother's milk. I was in Your care from birth. Since my mother gave birth to me, You have been my God. Do not be far from me.
PSALM 22:9–11 NLV

*God is my salvation; I will trust, and not be
afraid: for the LORD JEHOVAH is my strength
and my song; he also is become my salvation.*
ISAIAH 12:2 KJV

*"Whoever can be trusted with very
little can also be trusted with much."*
LUKE 16:10 NIV

*The hope of the man without God is destroyed.
What he trusts in is easy to break, like the home of
a spider. The spider trusts in his house, but it falls
apart. He holds on to it, but it does not hold.*
JOB 8:13–15 NLV

*The fear of man brings a snare,
but whoever trusts in the LORD shall be safe.*
PROVERBS 29:25 NKJV

*Trust in the Lord forever. For the
Lord God is a Rock that lasts forever.*
ISAIAH 26:4 NLV

And he hath put a new song in my mouth,
even praise unto our God: many shall see it,
and fear, and shall trust in the LORD.
PSALM 40:3 KJV

"For every breach of trust, whether it is for an ox,
for a donkey, for a sheep, for a cloak, or for any kind
of lost thing, of which one says, 'This is it,' the case
of both parties shall come before God. The one whom
God condemns shall pay double to his neighbor."
EXODUS 22:9 ESV

All you Israelites, trust in the LORD—he is their
help and shield. House of Aaron, trust in the
LORD—he is their help and shield. You who fear
him, trust in the LORD—he is their help and shield.
PSALM 115:9–11 NIV

Trust in the LORD with all your heart and lean
not on your own understanding; in all your ways
submit to him, and he will make your paths straight.
PROVERBS 3:5–6 NIV

*When they went out, Jehoshaphat stood and said,
"Listen to me, O Judah and people of Jerusalem.
Trust in the Lord your God, and you will be
made strong. Trust in the men who speak
for Him, and you will do well."*
2 Chronicles 20:20 nlv

*Our fathers trusted in You; they trusted, and You
delivered them. They cried to You, and were delivered;
they trusted in You, and were not ashamed.*
Psalm 22:4–5 nkjv

*"But he who sent me is trustworthy,
and what I have heard from him I tell the world."*
John 8:26 niv

*And again, "I will put my trust in him." And again,
"Behold, I and the children God has given me."*
Hebrews 2:13 esv

*And they that know thy name will put their
trust in thee: for thou, Lord, hast not
forsaken them that seek thee.*
Psalm 9:10 kjv

*Consider and answer me, O L*ORD *my God;*
light up my eyes, lest I sleep the sleep of death,
lest my enemy say, "I have prevailed over him,"
lest my foes rejoice because I am shaken. But I
have trusted in your steadfast love; my heart shall
*rejoice in your salvation. I will sing to the L*ORD,
because he has dealt bountifully with me.
PSALM 13:3–6 ESV

"You are happy when people act and talk in a bad
way to you and make it very hard for you and tell bad
things and lies about you because you trust in Me."
MATTHEW 5:11 NLV

*The L*ORD *is my rock and my fortress and my*
deliverer; my God, my strength, in whom I will
trust; my shield and the horn of my salvation,
my stronghold.
PSALM 18:2 NKJV

I want to trust, Lord. But I can't. I want to give You control over my life. But no matter how many times I say the words, I can't follow through on them. I feel stuck. I'm helpless to change. Lord, I know You can do the impossible. Work a miracle in my heart, I pray.

DIVORCE/SEPARATION

When a marriage fails, it hurts. Even if the relationship itself was unhealthy, the final breakup is painful. We are full of disappointment and sorrow. And we may feel embarrassment and resentment alongside our hurt. The future we had hoped for is gone, and we don't know what to hope for in its place.

All we can do is turn to God. In the midst of what seems like one of the biggest failures of our lives, He is there. He has not abandoned us. He still has plans for our lives. And His love for us will never fail.

Now the law came in to increase the trespass, but where sin increased, grace abounded all the more, so that, as sin reigned in death, grace also might reign through righteousness leading to eternal life through Jesus Christ our Lord.
ROMANS 5:20–21 ESV

To the married I give this command (not I, but the Lord): A wife must not separate from her husband. But if she does, she must remain unmarried or else be reconciled to her husband. And a husband must not divorce his wife. To the rest I say this (I, not the Lord): If any brother has a wife who is not a believer and she is willing to live with him, he must not divorce her. . . . But if the unbeliever leaves, let it be so. The brother or the sister is not bound in such circumstances; God has called us to live in peace.

1 CORINTHIANS 7:10–12, 15 NIV

"For the LORD God of Israel says that He hates divorce, for it covers one's garment with violence," says the LORD of hosts. "Therefore take heed to your spirit, that you do not deal treacherously."

MALACHI 2:16 NKJV

"The LORD will fight for you;
you need only to be still."
EXODUS 14:14 NIV

Blessed be God, even the Father of our Lord Jesus
Christ, the Father of mercies, and the God of all
comfort; who comforteth us in all our tribulation,
that we may be able to comfort them which are
in any trouble, by the comfort wherewith we
ourselves are comforted of God.
2 CORINTHIANS 1:3–4 KJV

To the Lord our God belong mercies and forgivenesses,
though we have rebelled against him.
DANIEL 9:9 KJV

The LORD appeared to us in the past, saying:
"I have loved you with an everlasting love;
I have drawn you with unfailing kindness.
I will build you up again, and you. . .
will be rebuilt. Again you will take up your
timbrels and go out to dance with the joyful."
JEREMIAH 31:3–4 NIV

"Fear not, for you will not be ashamed. Do not be troubled, for you will not be put to shame. You will forget how you were ashamed when you were young. You will not remember the sorrow of being without a husband any more. Your Maker is your husband. His name is the Lord of All. And the One Who saves you is the Holy One of Israel. He is called the God of All the earth. For the Lord has called you like a wife left alone and filled with sorrow, like a wife who married when young and is left," says your God. "For a short time I left you, but with much loving-pity I will take you back. When I was very angry I hid My face from you for a short time. But with loving-kindness that lasts forever I will have pity on you," says the Lord Who bought you and saves you.

ISAIAH 54:4–8 NLV

As for you, O LORD, you will not restrain your mercy from me; your steadfast love and your faithfulness will ever preserve me!

PSALM 40:11 ESV

I'm grieving today, Lord—grieving for the loss of companionship in my life, for the death of hopes, for broken promises, and for plans that will never be fulfilled. The pain I feel scares me. I'm afraid I can never recover from this wound. Give me courage to mourn my marriage. Give me strength to place it in Your loving hands and leave it there. Give me hope again. Heal my heart, I pray.

DOUBT

Peter was walking along on the surface of the water, his eyes fixed on Jesus, doing just fine. Suddenly, he realized what he was doing. He looked at the waves beneath his feet, and he knew that what he was doing was *impossible*. Instantly, he began to sink.

But Jesus didn't let him. Our Lord grabbed His good friend and saved him. And He does the same for us, over and over, every time we're swamped with doubts and start to sink into life's depths. "Why do you doubt Me?" He asks us. "Have I *ever* let you sink?"

So He said, "Come." And when Peter had come down out of the boat, he walked on the water to go to Jesus. But when he saw that the wind was boisterous, he was afraid; and beginning to sink he cried out, saying, "Lord, save me!" And immediately Jesus stretched out His hand and caught him, and said to him, "O you of little faith, why did you doubt?"
MATTHEW 14:29–31 NKJV

Let us hold fast the profession of our faith without wavering; (for he is faithful that promised.)
HEBREWS 10:23 KJV

And have mercy on those who doubt.
JUDE 1:22 ESV

But the wisdom that comes from heaven is first of all pure. Then it gives peace. It is gentle and willing to obey. It is full of loving-kindness and of doing good. It has no doubts and does not pretend to be something it is not.
JAMES 3:17 NLV

But when you ask, you must believe and not doubt, because the one who doubts is like a wave of the sea, blown and tossed by the wind.
JAMES 1:6 NIV

Abraham did not doubt God's promise. His faith in God was strong, and he gave thanks to God. He was sure God was able to do what He had promised.
ROMANS 4:20–21 NLV

*"Truly, I say to you, whoever says to this mountain,
'Be taken up and thrown into the sea,' and does not
doubt in his heart, but believes that what he says
will come to pass, it will be done for him."*

MARK 11:23 ESV

*The apostles said to the Lord, "Increase our faith!" And
the Lord said, "If you had faith like a grain of mustard
seed, you could say to this mulberry tree, 'Be uprooted
and planted in the sea,' and it would obey you."*

LUKE 17:5–6 ESV

*O Jacob and Israel, why do you say, "My way is
hidden from the Lord. My God does not think
about my cause"? Have you not known? Have you
not heard? The God Who lives forever is the Lord,
the One Who made the ends of the earth. He will
not become weak or tired. His understanding is
too great for us to begin to know.*

ISAIAH 40:27–28 NLV

*Arise therefore, and get thee down, and go with
them, doubting nothing: for I have sent them.*

ACTS 10:20 KJV

Jesus said to them, "Why are you afraid?
Why do you have doubts in your hearts?
Look at My hands and My feet. See! It is I,
Myself! Touch Me and see for yourself."
LUKE 24:38–39 NLV

Arise therefore, and get thee down, and go with
them, doubting nothing: for I have sent them.
ACTS 10:20 KJV

And when he saw a fig tree in the way, he came to
it, and found nothing thereon, but leaves only, and
said unto it, Let no fruit grow on thee henceforward
for ever. And presently the fig tree withered away.
And when the disciples saw it, they marvelled,
saying, How soon is the fig tree withered away!
Jesus answered and said unto them, Verily I say
unto you, If ye have faith, and doubt not, ye shall
not only do this which is done to the fig tree. . . .
All things, whatsoever ye shall ask in prayer,
believing, ye shall receive.
MATTHEW 21:19–22 KJV

*Take heed, brethren, lest there be in any of you
an evil heart of unbelief, in departing from
the living God. But exhort one another daily,
while it is called To day; lest any of you be
hardened through the deceitfulness of sin. For we
are made partakers of Christ, if we hold the
beginning of our confidence stedfast unto the end.*

HEBREWS 3:12–14 KJV

*Jesus, I can't help but identify with Peter—and with
Thomas, too. I want proof that You will keep Your
promises to me, that You are who You say You are,
that You will help me to do the things that seem so
impossible. Forgive me for doubting.*

DYSFUNCTIONAL RELATIONSHIPS

It's hard to cope with relationships that are broken. We keep hoping that despite the way things have gone in the past, *this time* things will be different.

We play our own role in these dysfunctional relationships. We may be an enabler, allowing the individuals involved to keep on doing things that hurt. Or we may get sucked into the fights and the hurtful habits.

But God wants to heal our entire lives, including our relationships. This healing is not likely to happen overnight—but our God can do amazing things. A miracle that takes time is still a miracle!

At my first trial no one helped me. Everyone left me. . . . But the Lord was with me.
2 TIMOTHY 4:16–17 NLV

Love is patient and kind; love does not envy or
boast; it is not arrogant or rude. It does not insist
on its own way; it is not irritable or resentful;
it does not rejoice at wrongdoing, but rejoices with
the truth. Love bears all things, believes all things,
hopes all things, endures all things.
1 CORINTHIANS 13:4–7 ESV

Therefore comfort each other and edify
one another, just as you also are doing.
1 THESSALONIANS 5:11 NKJV

Above all else, guard your heart,
for everything you do flows from it.
PROVERBS 4:23 NIV

Then Peter came up and said to him, "Lord, how often
will my brother sin against me, and I forgive him?
As many as seven times?" Jesus said to him, "I do not
say to you seven times, but seventy-seven times."
MATTHEW 18:21–22 ESV

He that troubleth his own
house shall inherit the wind.
PROVERBS 11:29 KJV

*Then Abram said to Lot, "Let there be no strife
between you and me, and between your herdsmen
and my herdsmen, for we are kinsmen. Is not the
whole land before you? Separate yourself from me.
If you take the left hand, then I will go to the right,
or if you take the right hand, then I will go to the
left." . . . The* LORD *said to Abram, after Lot had
separated from him, "Lift up your eyes and look
from the place where you are, northward
and southward and eastward and westward,
for all the land that you see I will give to you
and to your offspring forever."*
GENESIS 13:8–9, 14–15 ESV

*Live as free people, but do not use your freedom
as a cover-up for evil; live as God's slaves.
Show proper respect to everyone, love the
family of believers, fear God.*
1 PETER 2:16–17 NIV

*Where there is strife, there is pride,
but wisdom is found in those who take advice.*
PROVERBS 13:10 NIV

We have spoken to you who are in the city of Corinth with plain words. Our hearts are wide open. Our hearts are not closed to you. But you have closed your hearts to us. I am speaking to you now as if you were my own children. Open your hearts wide to us!

2 CORINTHIANS 6:11–13 NLV

Do nothing out of selfish ambition or vain conceit. Rather, in humility value others above yourselves, not looking to your own interests but each of you to the interests of the others. In your relationships with one another, have the same mindset as Christ Jesus. . . . Therefore God exalted him to the highest place and gave him the name that is above every name.

PHILIPPIANS 2:3–5, 9 NIV

There was a man sent from God whose name was John. He came as a witness to testify concerning that light, so that through him all might believe. He himself was not the light; he came only as a witness to the light.

JOHN 1:6–8 NIV

*Now may the God of patience and comfort
grant you to be like-minded toward one another,
according to Christ Jesus.*
ROMANS 15:5 NKJV

*Help each other. Speak day after day to each
other while it is still today so your heart will
not become hard by being fooled by sin. For we
belong to Christ if we keep on trusting Him
to the end just as we trusted Him at first.*
HEBREWS 3:13–14 NLV

*We love him, because he first loved us. If a man say,
I love God, and hateth his brother, he is a liar:
for he that loveth not his brother whom he hath
seen, how can he love God whom he hath not seen?
And this commandment have we from him,
That he who loveth God love his brother also.*
1 JOHN 4:19–21 KJV

Creator God, I focus so often on how I want others to change. I pray for them, I nag them, I lecture them, I beg them, I try to manipulate them. Ultimately, none of it does much good. Instead, God, show me where I need to change. I put myself into Your hands. I'm willing to have You do whatever it takes to heal my relationships.

Elderly Parents

Our parents' increasing needs seldom come at a time that's convenient for us. Instead, the season of life when we're the busiest with our own families and lives, doing our best to juggle all of life's growing demands, is the very time when our parents are likely to need more of our time and attention.

We may be surprised, though, to find that as our parents age, our changed relationship with them has its rewards as well. Our parents are not too old to offer us love and advice, if we can open our hearts to them. God will bless us through them—sometimes in surprising ways!

Children, obey your parents in the Lord, for this is right. "Honor your father and mother" (this is the first commandment with a promise), "that it may go well with you and that you may live long in the land."
Ephesians 6:1–3 esv

Let them first learn to show godliness to their own
household and to make some return to their parents,
for this is pleasing in the sight of God.
1 TIMOTHY 5:4 ESV

"Stand up in the presence of the aged, show respect
for the elderly and revere your God. I am the LORD."
LEVITICUS 19:32 NIV

Listen to your father, who gave you life, and do not
despise your mother when she is old. Buy the truth
and do not sell it—wisdom, instruction and insight
as well. The father of a righteous child has great joy;
a man who fathers a wise son rejoices in him.
May your father and mother rejoice;
may she who gave you birth be joyful!
PROVERBS 23:22–25 NIV

But if any provide not for his own, and specially
for those of his own house, he hath denied
the faith, and is worse than an infidel.
1 TIMOTHY 5:8 KJV

Behold, children are a heritage from the LORD,
the fruit of the womb a reward. Like arrows in the
hand of a warrior are the children of one's youth.
Blessed is the man who fills his quiver with them!
PSALM 127:3–5 ESV

The mother of Jesus and her sister Mary, the wife
of Cleophas, were standing near the cross. Mary
Magdalene was there also. Jesus saw His mother and
the follower whom He loved standing near. He said
to His mother, "Woman, look at your son." Then Jesus
said to the follower, "Look at your mother." From
that time the follower took her to his own house.
JOHN 19:25–27 NLV

"Listen to me, you descendants of Jacob, all the
remnant of the people of Israel, you whom I have
upheld since your birth, and have carried since you
were born. Even to your old age and gray hairs
I am he, I am he who will sustain you. I have
made you and I will carry you; I will sustain
you and I will rescue you."
ISAIAH 46:3–4 NIV

Gray hair is a crown of glory;
it is gained in a righteous life.
PROVERBS 16:31 ESV

Jesus said to Peter the second time, "Simon,
son of John, do you love Me?" He answered Jesus,
"Yes, Lord, You know that I love You."
Jesus said to him, "Take care of My sheep."
JOHN 21:16 NLV

Then the women said to Naomi, "Blessed be the
LORD, who has not left you this day without
a close relative; and may his name be famous
in Israel! And may he be to you a restorer of
life and a nourisher of your old age."
RUTH 4:14–15 NKJV

The righteous shall flourish like a palm tree,
he shall grow like a cedar in Lebanon. Those who
are planted in the house of the LORD shall flourish
in the courts of our God. They shall still bear fruit
in old age; they shall be fresh and flourishing.
PSALM 92:12–14 NKJV

Bear one another's burdens,
and so fulfill the law of Christ.
GALATIANS 6:2 NKJV

My son, keep your father's command, and do
not forsake the law of your mother. Bind them
continually upon your heart; tie them around
your neck. When you roam, they will lead you;
when you sleep, they will keep you; and when
you awake, they will speak with you. For the
commandment is a lamp, and the law a light;
reproofs of instruction are the way of life.
PROVERBS 6:20–23 NKJV

You know how busy I am, Lord. It's hard for me to
sort out the demands on my time. Show me what
my priorities should be. Give me wisdom to know
how to help my parents as they age.

ENEMIES

We make enemies out of the people we don't approve of, the people who disagree with what we believe, who have different politics, different values, different agendas. We might deny that we treat them like enemies—but do we act as though we love them? Do we give them our best? Do we pray for them with all our energy?

Jesus tells us that we can't be His mature followers—in fact, we can't even realize our own God-given identities—if we don't start treating everyone, including our enemies, with the same grace and generosity God has shown us.

"But love your enemies, and do good, and lend, expecting nothing in return, and your reward will be great, and you will be sons of the Most High, for he is kind to the ungrateful and the evil. Be merciful, even as your Father is merciful."
LUKE 6:35–36 ESV

119

All my bones will say, "Lord, who is like You?
Who saves the weak from those too strong for them?
Who saves the poor from those who would rob
them?" People come telling lies. . . . They pay me
what is bad in return for what is good. My soul is
sad. But when they were sick, I put on clothes made
from hair. With no pride in my soul, I would not
eat. And I prayed with my head on my chest.
PSALM 35:10–13 NLV

For thou hast been a shelter for me,
and a strong tower from the enemy.
PSALM 61:3 KJV

When the LORD takes pleasure in anyone's way,
he causes their enemies to make peace with them.
PROVERBS 16:7 NIV

Through God we shall do valiantly:
for he it is that shall tread down our enemies.
PSALM 60:12 KJV

[The LORD] freed us from our enemies.
His love endures forever.
PSALM 136:24 NIV

David himself, in the Holy Spirit, declared,
"The Lord said to my Lord, 'Sit at my right hand,
until I put your enemies under your feet.'"
MARK 12:36 ESV

Jesus said, "Father, forgive them,
for they do not know what they are doing."
LUKE 23:34 NIV

For if, when we were enemies, we were reconciled
to God by the death of his Son, much more,
being reconciled, we shall be saved by his life.
And not only so, but we also joy in God through
our Lord Jesus Christ, by whom we have
now received the atonement.
ROMANS 5:10–11 KJV

"Have I been glad when a person who hated me
was destroyed? Have I been filled with joy when
trouble came to him? No, I have not allowed my
mouth to sin by asking his life to be cursed."
JOB 31:29–30 NLV

Because of his strength will I wait
upon thee: for God is my defence.
PSALM 59:9 KJV

If your enemy is hungry, give him bread to eat,
and if he is thirsty, give him water to drink,
for you will heap burning coals on his head,
and the LORD will reward you.
PROVERBS 25:21–22 ESV

"You have heard that it was said, 'You shall love
your neighbor and hate your enemy.' But I say to
you, love your enemies, bless those who curse you,
do good to those who hate you, and pray for those
who spitefully use you and persecute you, that you
may be sons of your Father in heaven; for He makes
His sun rise on the evil and on the good, and sends
rain on the just and on the unjust. For if you love
those who love you, what reward have you?"
MATTHEW 5:43–46 NKJV

Lead me, O LORD, in Your righteousness because of
my enemies; make Your way straight before my face.
PSALM 5:8 NKJV

122

But ye, brethren, be not weary in well doing.
And if any man obey not our word by this epistle,
note that man, and have no company with him,
that he may be ashamed. Yet count him not as an
enemy, but admonish him as a brother. Now the
Lord of peace himself give you peace always by
all means. The Lord be with you all.

2 THESSALONIANS 3:13–16 KJV

Holy Spirit, fill me with Your love. Help me to love
not only You, but all those whom You have created.
Teach me not to be so sensitive to slights and insults.
Help me to focus always on what is good for others
rather than myself. Teach me to love as You love.

Facing Death

The closer death comes to us, the harder it may be for us to hold on to our confidence in eternal life. Is there really anything beyond death? Or will all that we are cease to exist once we stop breathing?

The Bible assures us that physical death is not the end. Jesus came to this earth so that our fears could be put to rest. He has promised us that He has prepared a place for us in the life to come—and when we die, we will hear His voice welcoming us into the eternal celebration.

Even if I walk through the valley of the shadow of death, I will not be afraid of anything, because You are with me.
PSALM 23:4 NLV

For this is God, our God forever and ever; He will be our guide even to death.
PSALM 48:14 NKJV

So when this corruptible shall have put on
incorruption, and this mortal shall have put on
immortality, then shall be brought to pass the
saying that is written, Death is swallowed up
in victory. O death, where is thy sting?
O grave, where is thy victory?
1 CORINTHIANS 15:54–55 KJV

Since the children have flesh and blood, he too shared
in their humanity so that by his death he might
break the power of him who holds the power of
death—that is, the devil—and free those who all
their lives were held in slavery by their fear of death.
HEBREWS 2:14–15 NIV

Jesus said unto her, I am the resurrection,
and the life: he that believeth in me,
though he were dead, yet shall he live.
JOHN 11:25 KJV

And he said, "Jesus, remember me when you come
into your kingdom." And he said to him, "Truly, I
say to you, today you will be with me in Paradise."
LUKE 23:42–43 ESV

The life of mortals is like grass, they flourish like a flower of the field; the wind blows over it and it is gone, and its place remembers it no more. But from everlasting to everlasting the LORD's love is with those who fear him.
PSALM 103:15–17 NIV

"I will deliver this people from the power of the grave; I will redeem them from death. Where, O death, are your plagues? Where, O grave, is your destruction?"
HOSEA 13:14 NIV

Just as people are destined to die once, and after that to face judgment, so Christ was sacrificed once to take away the sins of many; and he will appear a second time, not to bear sin, but to bring salvation to those who are waiting for him.
HEBREWS 9:27–28 NIV

My flesh and my heart fail; but God is the strength of my heart and my portion forever.
PSALM 73:26 NKJV

"Do not be afraid of what you will suffer. . . .
Be faithful even to death. Then I will give you the
crown of life. You have ears! Then listen to what the
Spirit says to the churches. The person who has power
and wins will not be hurt by the second death!"

REVELATION 2:10–11 NLV

When calamity comes, the wicked are brought down,
but even in death the righteous seek refuge in God.

PROVERBS 14:32 NIV

As no one has power over the wind to contain it,
so no one has power over the time of their death.

ECCLESIASTES 8:8 NIV

"O LORD, make me know my end and what is
the measure of my days; let me know how fleeting
I am! Behold, you have made my days a few
handbreadths, and my lifetime is as nothing before
you. . . . And now, O Lord, for what do I wait?
My hope is in you."

PSALM 39:4–5, 7 ESV

"For sure, I tell you, if anyone keeps My Word, that one will never die."
JOHN 8:51 NLV

(For we walk by faith, not by sight:) We are confident, I say, and willing rather to be absent from the body, and to be present with the Lord.
2 CORINTHIANS 5:7–8 KJV

We know about it now because of the coming of Jesus Christ, the One Who saves. He put a stop to the power of death and brought life that never dies which is seen through the Good News.
2 TIMOTHY 1:10 NLV

Our God is a God of salvation, and to GOD, the Lord, belong deliverances from death.
PSALM 68:20 ESV

Jesus, when I read about Your death on the cross, I can tell You went through much of what I'm experiencing now. You felt lonely and forsaken. You wondered where God was. You felt death's pain and horror. And yet in the midst of all that, You still trusted Your Father. You put Your spirit in His hands. God, I want to follow Your Son's example. I commit my spirit into Your hands.

FAILURE

Theodore Roosevelt once said something along these lines: "The only person who never makes a mistake—who never experiences failure—is the person who never does anything."

Even the great heroes of our Christian faith experienced their share of failure. Abraham and Moses, Elijah and David, Peter and Paul—they all knew what it was like to make serious mistakes. But God used even their failures to bring them to the place where He wanted them to be.

No matter how many times we fail, His love never does. And in the midst of our failures, we can still find victory in Christ.

For we all stumble in many things.
JAMES 3:2 NKJV

Humble yourselves before the Lord,
and he will lift you up.
JAMES 4:10 NIV

But he said to me, "My grace is sufficient for you, for my power is made perfect in weakness." Therefore I will boast all the more gladly of my weaknesses, so that the power of Christ may rest upon me. For the sake of Christ, then, I am content with weaknesses, insults, hardships, persecutions, and calamities. For when I am weak, then I am strong.

2 CORINTHIANS 12:9–10 ESV

"You shall say to them, Thus says the LORD: When men fall, do they not rise again? If one turns away, does he not return? Why then has this people turned away in perpetual backsliding? They hold fast to deceit; they refuse to return."

JEREMIAH 8:4–5 ESV

Two are better than one, because they have a good reward for their labor. For if they fall, one will lift up his companion. But woe to him who is alone when he falls, for he has no one to help him up.

ECCLESIASTES 4:9–10 NKJV

Therefore, if anyone is in Christ, the new creation has come: The old has gone, the new is here!

2 CORINTHIANS 5:17 NIV

*If we confess our sins, he is faithful and
just to forgive us our sins and to cleanse
us from all unrighteousness.*
1 JOHN 1:9 ESV

*And now why tarriest thou? arise,
and be baptized, and wash away thy sins,
calling on the name of the Lord.*
ACTS 22:16 KJV

*The LORD makes firm the steps of the one who
delights in him; though he may stumble, he will
not fall, for the LORD upholds him with his hand.*
PSALM 37:23–24 NIV

*"Yours, O LORD, is the greatness and the power
and the glory and the victory and the majesty,
for all that is in the heavens and in the earth is
yours. Yours is the kingdom, O LORD, and you are
exalted as head above all. Both riches and honor
come from you, and you rule over all. In your hand
are power and might, and in your hand it is to
make great and to give strength to all."*
1 CHRONICLES 29:11–12 ESV

For a righteous man may fall seven times and rise again, but the wicked shall fall by calamity.

PROVERBS 24:16 NKJV

Cast your burden on the LORD, and he will sustain you; he will never permit the righteous to be moved.

PSALM 55:22 ESV

And we know that all things work together for good to those who love God, to those who are the called according to His purpose. For whom He foreknew, He also predestined to be conformed to the image of His Son, that He might be the firstborn among many brethren.

ROMANS 8:28–29 NKJV

The LORD upholdeth all that fall, and raiseth up all those that be bowed down.

PSALM 145:14 KJV

He drew me up from the pit of destruction, out of the miry bog, and set my feet upon a rock, making my steps secure. He put a new song in my mouth, a song of praise to our God.

PSALM 40:2–3 ESV

I do not say that I have received this or have already become perfect. But I keep going on to make that life my own as Christ Jesus made me His own. No, Christian brothers, I do not have that life yet. But I do one thing. I forget everything that is behind me and look forward to that which is ahead of me. My eyes are on the crown.
PHILIPPIANS 3:12–14 NLV

Teach me, Lord, to find You even in the midst of failure. Let me never put off holding out my arms to You so that You can pick me up and put me back on my feet. Thank You that Your grace never fails.

Fear

Fear is a normal and healthy biological reaction that alerts us to danger. Unfortunately, in our lives, fear and danger no longer necessarily go together. Instead, fear can exist all on its own. When that happens, fear becomes destructive and crippling. As Franklin D. Roosevelt said, "The only thing we have to fear is fear itself."

When we find ourselves in bondage to fear, God holds the key that can set us free. When life seems threatening, filled with unknown (and possibly imaginary) dangers, He will be our refuge. He is always there. In Him we can always be secure.

"But whoever listens to me will dwell secure and will be at ease, without dread of disaster."
PROVERBS 1:33 ESV

"So do not fear, for I am with you; do not be dismayed, for I am your God."
ISAIAH 41:10 NIV

So that we may boldly say, The Lord is my helper,
and I will not fear what man shall do unto me.
HEBREWS 13:6 KJV

For God did not give us a spirit of fear. He gave us
a spirit of power and of love and of a good mind.
2 TIMOTHY 1:7 NLV

Fear not, little flock; for it is your Father's
good pleasure to give you the kingdom.
LUKE 12:32 KJV

"Are not five sparrows sold for two copper coins?
And not one of them is forgotten before God.
But the very hairs of your head are all numbered.
Do not fear therefore; you are of more value
than many sparrows."
LUKE 12:6–7 NKJV

The fear of man bringeth a snare: but whoso
putteth his trust in the LORD shall be safe.
PROVERBS 29:25 KJV

*"And do not fear those who kill the body but
cannot kill the soul. But rather fear Him who
is able to destroy both soul and body in hell."*
MATTHEW 10:28 NKJV

*Fear and trembling come upon me, and horror
overwhelms me. And I say, "Oh, that I had wings
like a dove! I would fly away and be at rest; yes,
I would wander far away; I would lodge in the
wilderness; I would hurry to find a shelter from the
raging wind and tempest.". . . But I call to God,
and the LORD will save me. Evening and morning
and at noon I utter my complaint and moan,
and he hears my voice.*
PSALM 55:5–8, 16–17 ESV

*"Peace I leave with you; my peace I give you.
I do not give to you as the world gives. Do not
let your hearts be troubled and do not be afraid."*
JOHN 14:27 NIV

*I sought the LORD, and He heard me,
and delivered me from all my fears.*
PSALM 34:4 NKJV

The LORD is my light and my salvation—
whom shall I fear? The LORD is the stronghold
of my life—of whom shall I be afraid?
PSALM 27:1 NIV

Do not be afraid of sudden terror, nor of trouble from
the wicked when it comes; for the LORD will be your
confidence, and will keep your foot from being caught.
PROVERBS 3:25–26 NKJV

When thou liest down, thou shalt not be afraid: yea,
thou shalt lie down, and thy sleep shall be sweet.
PROVERBS 3:24 KJV

God is our safe place and our strength. He is
always our help when we are in trouble. So we
will not be afraid, even if the earth is shaken and
the mountains fall into the center of the sea,
and even if its waters go wild with storm
and the mountains shake with its action.
PSALM 46:1–3 NLV

He laid His right hand on me and said, "Do not be afraid. I am the First and the Last. I am the Living One. I was dead, but look, I am alive forever."

REVELATION 1:17–18 NLV

The Spirit you received does not make you slaves, so that you live in fear again; rather, the Spirit you received brought about your adoption to sonship. And by him we cry, "Abba, Father."

ROMANS 8:15 NIV

And it shall come to pass in the day that the LORD shall give thee rest from thy sorrow, and from thy fear, and from the hard bondage wherein thou wast made to serve.

ISAIAH 14:3 KJV

For I, the LORD your God, hold your right hand; it is I who say to you, "Fear not, I am the one who helps you."

ISAIAH 41:13 ESV

✳

*Thank You, Jesus, that You have given me Your peace.
I know Your peace is not like anything the world has
to offer me. Because of You, I will not let my heart be
troubled, neither will I let it be afraid (see John 14:27).*

FINANCES

God uses our financial needs to draw us closer
to Him. He hasn't promised that we will be
rich, nor does He demand that we be penniless.
Instead, He wants us to simply trust Him,
whatever our finances. Even in the midst of
financial stress, He offers us the prosperity and
abundance of His grace. He has promised to
meet our every need.

But my God shall supply all your need
according to his riches in glory by Christ Jesus.
PHILIPPIANS 4:19 KJV

What is more, I consider everything a loss because
of the surpassing worth of knowing Christ Jesus
my Lord, for whose sake I have lost all things.
I consider them garbage, that I may gain Christ.
PHILIPPIANS 3:8 NIV

Owe no one anything except to love one another.
ROMANS 13:8 NKJV

"For the holy nation of heaven is like a man who was going to a country far away. He called together the servants he owned and gave them his money to use. . . . The servant who had the five pieces of money went out to the stores and traded until he made five more pieces. . . . After a long time the owner of those servants came back. He wanted to know what had been done with his money. The one who had received the five pieces of money worth much came and handed him five pieces more. . . . His owner said to him, 'You have done well. You are a good and faithful servant. You have been faithful over a few things. I will put many things in your care. Come and share my joy.'"

MATTHEW 25:14, 16, 19–21 NLV

Command those who are rich in this present age not to be haughty, nor to trust in uncertain riches but in the living God, who gives us richly all things to enjoy. Let them do good, that they be rich in good works, ready to give, willing to share.

1 TIMOTHY 6:17–18 NKJV

Everyone also to whom God has given wealth and possessions and power to enjoy them, and to accept his lot and rejoice in his toil—this is the gift of God.
ECCLESIASTES 5:19 ESV

"Do not lay up for yourselves treasures on earth, where moth and rust destroy and where thieves break in and steal, but lay up for yourselves treasures in heaven, where neither moth nor rust destroys and where thieves do not break in and steal. For where your treasure is, there your heart will be also."
MATTHEW 6:19–21 ESV

"Do not keep saying, 'What will we eat?' or, 'What will we drink?' or, 'What will we wear?' The people who do not know God are looking for all these things. Your Father in heaven knows you need all these things. First of all, look for the holy nation of God. Be right with Him. All these other things will be given to you also."
MATTHEW 6:31–33 NLV

Praise the Lord! How happy is the man who honors
the Lord with fear and finds joy in His Law! . . .
Riches and well-being are in his house. And his
right-standing with God will last forever.
PSALM 112:1, 3 NLV

But godliness with contentment is great gain.
For we brought nothing into the world, and we
can take nothing out of it. But if we have food
and clothing, we will be content with that.
Those who want to get rich fall into temptation
and a trap and into many foolish and harmful
desires that plunge people into ruin and destruction.
For the love of money is a root of all kinds of evil.
Some people, eager for money, have wandered from
the faith and pierced themselves with many griefs.
But you, man of God, flee from all this, and pursue
righteousness, godliness, faith, love, endurance
and gentleness. Fight the good fight of the faith.
Take hold of. . .eternal life.
1 TIMOTHY 6:6–12 NIV

Honor the LORD with your wealth, with the firstfruits of all your crops; then your barns will be filled to overflowing, and your vats will brim over with new wine.

PROVERBS 3:9–10 NIV

Teach me, Jesus, to be content in whatever financial situation I find myself. Teach me how to have next to nothing—and how to have more than enough. In any and every financial circumstance, teach me the secret of facing either plenty or hunger, abundance or need. I believe You will supply my every need from Your riches in glory (see Philippians 4:11–13, 19).

GREED

Greed is the urge to get more and more of something, whether it be money or food or possessions. The greedy person is too attached to the things of this world. And as a result, the greedy person is often anxious, worried about losing what he already has.

The generous person, however, is truly free. She can open her hands and take the good things God brings into her life. And she can just as easily open her hands and let them go. Sharing brings her joy, and loss doesn't worry her. She knows that God has plenty to give her and His grace will never be exhausted.

Then Jesus said to them all, "Watch yourselves! Keep from wanting all kinds of things you should not have. A man's life is not made up of things, even if he has many riches."
LUKE 12:15 NLV

Remember the words of the Lord Jesus,
how he himself said, "It is more blessed
to give than to receive."
ACTS 20:35 ESV

The generous soul will be made rich, and he
who waters will also be watered himself.
PROVERBS 11:25 NKJV

If I give all I possess to the poor and give
over my body to hardship that I may boast,
but do not have love, I gain nothing.
1 CORINTHIANS 13:3 NIV

Each of you should give what you have decided
in your heart to give, not reluctantly or under
compulsion, for God loves a cheerful giver.
2 CORINTHIANS 9:7 NIV

Give generously to them and do so without a
grudging heart; then because of this the LORD
your God will bless you in all your work and
in everything you put your hand to.
DEUTERONOMY 15:10 NIV

*A man ran up and knelt before him and asked him,
"Good Teacher, what must I do to inherit eternal
life?" . . . And Jesus, looking at him, loved him,
and said to him, "You lack one thing: go,
sell all that you have and give to the poor, and you
will have treasure in heaven; and come, follow
me." Disheartened by the saying, he went away
sorrowful, for he had great possessions.*
MARK 10:17, 21–22 ESV

*"Do not lay up for yourselves treasures on earth,
where moth and rust destroy and where thieves
break in and steal; but lay up for yourselves treasures
in heaven, where neither moth nor rust destroys and
where thieves do not break in and steal. For where
your treasure is, there your heart will be also."*
MATTHEW 6:19–21 NKJV

*It is well with the man who deals generously
and lends; who conducts his affairs with justice. . . .
He has distributed freely; he has given to the poor;
his righteousness endures forever; his horn is
exalted in honor.*
PSALM 112:5, 9 ESV

Honor the Lord with your riches, and with the first of all you grow. Then your store-houses will be filled with many good things and your barrels will flow over with new wine.

PROVERBS 3:9–10 NLV

Those who give to the poor will lack nothing, but those who close their eyes to them receive many curses.

PROVERBS 28:27 NIV

Give, and it shall be given unto you; good measure, pressed down, and shaken together, and running over, shall men give into your bosom. For with the same measure that ye mete withal it shall be measured to you again.

LUKE 6:38 KJV

"So now, our God, we thank You. We praise Your great and honored name. But who am I and who are my people, that we should be able to give so much? For all things come from You. We have given You only what already belongs to You."

1 CHRONICLES 29:13–14 NLV

*Show me, God, that greed weighs me down. It doesn't give
me joy. Instead, when greed rules my heart, I am never
satisfied. Nothing is ever enough. I can't enjoy what I
have, because I'm too focused on what I don't have.*

HELPLESSNESS

We've all heard the expression "God helps those who help themselves." And while there's a certain truth to the saying, the opposite is also true: God helps those who are helpless.

In Jesus' day, the Pharisees didn't see themselves as helpless. They trusted in their own righteousness, in their own abilities to save themselves. But Jesus said, "Blessed are the poor in spirit, for theirs is the kingdom of heaven" (Matthew 5:3 NIV). When we are helpless, when we give up our dependence on our own strength, then God can begin to act in our lives.

I can do all things through
Christ who strengthens me.
PHILIPPIANS 4:13 NKJV

Arise, LORD! Lift up your hand, O God.
Do not forget the helpless. . . .
You are the helper of the fatherless.
PSALM 10:12, 14 NIV

151

*I have been crucified with Christ and I no longer
live, but Christ lives in me. The life I now live
in the body, I live by faith in the Son of God,
who loved me and gave himself for me.*

GALATIANS 2:20 NIV

*We are hard pressed on every side, but not crushed;
perplexed, but not in despair; persecuted, but not
abandoned; struck down, but not destroyed.*

2 CORINTHIANS 4:8–9 NIV

*"Then I will ask My Father and He will give you
another Helper. He will be with you forever. . . .
The Helper is the Holy Spirit. The Father will send
Him in My place. He will teach you everything
and help you remember everything I have told you."*

JOHN 14:16, 26 NLV

*In the same way, the Spirit helps us in our
weakness. We do not know what we ought
to pray for, but the Spirit himself intercedes
for us through wordless groans.*

ROMANS 8:26 NIV

You see, at just the right time, when we were still powerless, Christ died for the ungodly. Very rarely will anyone die for a righteous person, though for a good person someone might possibly dare to die. But God demonstrates his own love for us in this: While we were still sinners, Christ died for us.

ROMANS 5:6–8 NIV

For his sake I have suffered the loss of all things and count them as rubbish, in order that I may gain Christ and be found in him, not having a righteousness of my own that comes from the law, but that which comes through faith in Christ, the righteousness from God that depends on faith.

PHILIPPIANS 3:8–9 ESV

Humble yourselves in the sight of the Lord, and he shall lift you up.

JAMES 4:10 KJV

"Those who know there is nothing good in themselves are happy, because the holy nation of heaven is theirs."

MATTHEW 5:3 NLV

For we do not want you to be unaware, brothers, of the affliction we experienced in Asia. For we were so utterly burdened beyond our strength that we despaired of life itself. Indeed, we felt that we had received the sentence of death. But that was to make us rely not on ourselves but on God who raises the dead. He delivered us from such a deadly peril, and he will deliver us. On him we have set our hope.
2 Corinthians 1:8–10 esv

But the righteousness that is by faith says: "Do not say in your heart, 'Who will ascend into heaven?'" (that is, to bring Christ down) "or 'Who will descend into the deep?'" (that is, to bring Christ up from the dead). But what does it say? "The word is near you; it is in your mouth and in your heart."
Romans 10:6–8 niv

If I must boast, I will boast of the things that show my weakness.
2 Corinthians 11:30 niv

An argument arose among them as to which of them was the greatest. But Jesus, knowing the reasoning of their hearts, took a child and put him by his side and said to them, "Whoever receives this child in my name receives me, and whoever receives me receives him who sent me. For he who is least among you all is the one who is great."

LUKE 9:46–48 ESV

God, give me a healthy humility that depends on Your strength as my help and refuge. May my sense of helplessness not be based on lies I tell myself, however. When I hear myself saying things like, "There's no way I can get out of this mess," or "Life hasn't been fair to me, so why should I even try anymore?" remind me that these words are not the truth. Give me the courage that's based on confidence in Your strength.

Hidden Sin

Sin that is hidden still gets in the way of our relationship with God. By hiding it out of sight, we may think we have fooled other people. We may even fool ourselves. We do not fool God.

In the New Testament, Paul makes it clear that our hidden thoughts are just as serious and damaging as our external behaviors. He wants us to be people of integrity and wholeness, without any darkness festering inside us. He knows that ultimately our own selves are hurt the most by these shameful secrets.

Woe unto them that seek deep to hide their counsel from the LORD, and their works are in the dark, and they say, Who seeth us? and who knoweth us?
ISAIAH 29:15 KJV

The night is far spent, the day is at hand. Therefore let us cast off the works of darkness, and let us put on the armor of light.
ROMANS 13:12 NKJV

"For nothing is hidden except to be made manifest;
nor is anything secret except to come to light."
MARK 4:22 ESV

You have set our iniquities before you,
our secret sins in the light of your presence.
PSALM 90:8 ESV

No one who abides in him keeps on sinning;
no one who keeps on sinning has either
seen him or known him.
1 JOHN 3:6 ESV

Whoever conceals their sins does not prosper, but the
one who confesses and renounces them finds mercy.
PROVERBS 28:13 NIV

If we claim to be without sin, we deceive ourselves
and the truth is not in us. If we confess our sins,
he is faithful and just and will forgive us our sins
and purify us from all unrighteousness.
1 JOHN 1:8–9 NIV

No one can hide from God. His eyes see everything
we do. We must give an answer to God for what
we have done. We have a great Religious Leader
Who has made the way for man to go to God. He is
Jesus, the Son of God, Who has gone to heaven to
be with God. Let us keep our trust in Jesus Christ.
Our Religious Leader understands how weak
we are. Christ was tempted in every way we are
tempted, but He did not sin. Let us go with
complete trust to the throne of God. We will
receive His loving-kindness and have His
loving-favor to help us whenever we need it.
HEBREWS 4:13–16 NLV

The sins of some men can be seen. Their sins
go before them and make them guilty.
The sins of other men will be seen later.
1 TIMOTHY 5:24 NLV

"My eyes are on all their ways; they are not hidden
from me, nor is their sin concealed from my eyes."
JEREMIAH 16:17 NIV

*And they heard the sound of the LORD God walking
in the garden in the cool of the day, and the man
and his wife hid themselves from the presence of the
LORD God among the trees of the garden.
But the LORD God called to the man and said to
him, "Where are you?" And he said, "I heard the
sound of you in the garden, and I was afraid,
because I was naked, and I hid myself." He said,
"Who told you that you were naked? Have you eaten
of the tree of which I commanded you not to eat?"*
GENESIS 3:8–11 ESV

*When I kept silent, my bones grew old through
my groaning all the day long. For day and night
Your hand was heavy upon me; my vitality was
turned into the drought of summer. I acknowledged
my sin to You, and my iniquity I have not hidden.
I said, "I will confess my transgressions to the
LORD," and You forgave the iniquity of my sin.*
PSALM 32:3–5 NKJV

*O God, You know my foolishness;
and my sins are not hidden from You.*
PSALM 69:5 NKJV

"Have I hidden my sins like Adam? Have I hidden my wrong-doing in my heart. . . . If only I had one to hear me! See, here my name is written. Let the All-powerful answer me! May what is against me be written down! For sure I would carry it on my shoulder. I would tie it around my head like a crown. I would tell Him the number of my every step. I would come near Him like a prince."
JOB 31:33, 35–37 NLV

Teach me, Lord, never to be dishonest with myself or You. Examine my heart, and reveal its contents. May there be no secrets between us.

HOPELESSNESS

We tend to think of hope as a cheery, optimistic outlook on life. But the biblical concept of hope is far greater and deeper. It is a confidence and expectation in what God will do in the future, an understanding that the same God who was with us yesterday will be with us tomorrow.

When things seem hopeless, we are robbed of this confidence. We feel as though the future is empty and barren. But hopelessness is always a lie, for our God has big plans for us! No matter how hard the road, it always leads us into His presence.

Our hope comes from God. May He fill you with joy and peace because of your trust in Him. May your hope grow stronger by the power of the Holy Spirit.
ROMANS 15:13 NLV

For God alone, O my soul, wait in silence, for my hope is from him.
PSALM 62:5 ESV

Be joyful in hope, patient in affliction,
faithful in prayer.
Romans 12:12 niv

Blessed be the God and Father of our Lord Jesus
Christ, who according to His abundant mercy
has begotten us again to a living hope through the
resurrection of Jesus Christ from the dead, to an
inheritance incorruptible and undefiled and that
does not fade away, reserved in heaven for you,
who are kept by the power of God through faith
for salvation ready to be revealed in the last time.
In this you greatly rejoice, though now for a little
while, if need be, you have been grieved by various
trials, that the genuineness of your faith, being
much more precious than gold that perishes, though
it is tested by fire, may be found to praise, honor,
and glory at the revelation of Jesus Christ.
1 Peter 1:3–7 nkjv

Thou art my hiding place and my shield:
I hope in thy word.
Psalm 119:114 kjv

"For I know the plans I have for you," says the Lord,
"plans for well-being and not for trouble,
to give you a future and a hope."
JEREMIAH 29:11 NLV

Life will be brighter than noonday,
and darkness will become like morning.
You will be secure, because there is hope.
JOB 11:17–18 NIV

"You wearied yourself by such going about,
but you would not say, 'It is hopeless.' You found
renewal of your strength, and so you did not faint."
ISAIAH 57:10 NIV

"For there is hope for a tree, if it is cut down,
that it will sprout again, and that
its tender shoots will not cease."
JOB 14:7 NKJV

In hope he believed against hope, that he
should become the father of many nations,
as he had been told, "So shall your offspring be."
ROMANS 4:18 ESV

We rejoice in our sufferings, knowing that suffering produces endurance, and endurance produces character, and character produces hope, and hope does not put us to shame, because God's love has been poured into our hearts through the Holy Spirit who has been given to us.
Romans 5:3–5 esv

"In His name the nations will have hope."
Matthew 12:21 nlv

Why art thou cast down, O my soul? and why art thou disquieted in me? hope thou in God: for I shall yet praise him for the help of his countenance.
Psalm 42:5 kjv

Everything that has been made in the world is weak. It is not that the world wanted it to be that way. God allowed it to be that way. Yet there is hope.
Romans 8:20 nlv

Hope deferred makes the heart sick, but when the desire comes, it is a tree of life.
Proverbs 13:12 nkjv

*If in Christ we have hope in this life only,
we are of all people most to be pitied. But in
fact Christ has been raised from the dead, the
firstfruits of those who have fallen asleep. For as
by a man came death, by a man has come also the
resurrection of the dead. For as in Adam all die,
so also in Christ shall all be made alive.*
1 Corinthians 15:19–22 esv

*We were saved with this hope ahead of us.
Now hope means we are waiting for something we
do not have. How can a man hope for something he
already has? But if we hope for something we do not
yet see, we must learn how to wait for it.*
Romans 8:24–25 nlv

*Now may our Lord Jesus Christ himself, and God
our Father, who loved us and gave us eternal comfort
and good hope through grace, comfort your hearts
and establish them in every good work and word.*
2 Thessalonians 2:16–17 esv

INFERTILITY

When you can't become pregnant, you may feel as though you are unworthy, worthless. Even in this day of women's rights, you may still believe that your value, your personhood, your fulfillment all depend on your ability to have a child.

God wants you to beware of this lie. When we become obsessed with wanting something—no matter how good it might be—we turn it into a god. Our value comes from God alone—and we can trust Him to fulfill the deepest longings of our hearts in the way that is best for us.

For in Him dwells all the fullness of the Godhead bodily; and you are complete in Him.
Colossians 2:9–10 NKJV

And he said unto me,
My grace is sufficient for thee.
2 Corinthians 12:9 KJV

Therefore I say to you, whatever things you ask when you pray, believe that you receive them, and you will have them.
MARK 11:24 NKJV

And Isaac prayed to the LORD for his wife, because she was barren. And the LORD granted his prayer, and Rebekah his wife conceived.
GENESIS 25:21 ESV

O Lord, all my longing is before you; my sighing is not hidden from you. . . . But for you, O LORD, do I wait; it is you, O Lord my God, who will answer.
PSALM 38:9, 15 ESV

Your eyes saw me before I was put together. And all the days of my life were written in Your book before any of them came to be. Your thoughts are of great worth to me, O God. How many there are! If I could number them, there would be more than the sand. When I awake, I am still with You.
PSALM 139:16–18 NLV

"See, your cousin Elizabeth, as old as she is, is going to give birth to a child. She was not able to have children before, but now she is in her sixth month. For God can do all things."

LUKE 1:36–37 NLV

"Be glad, barren woman, you who never bore a child; shout for joy and cry aloud, you who were never in labor; because more are the children of the desolate woman than of her who has a husband."

GALATIANS 4:27 NIV

Though the fig tree may not blossom, nor fruit be on the vines; though the labor of the olive may fail, and the fields yield no food; though the flock may be cut off from the fold, and there be no herd in the stalls—yet I will rejoice in the LORD, I will joy in the God of my salvation.

HABAKKUK 3:17–18 NKJV

You will remember all the way the Lord your God led you in the desert these forty years, so you would not have pride, and how He tested you to know what was in your heart.

DEUTERONOMY 8:2 NLV

And by faith even Sarah, who was past childbearing age, was enabled to bear children because she considered him faithful who had made the promise.
HEBREWS 11:11 NIV

Satisfy us in the morning with your unfailing love, that we may sing for joy and be glad all our days. Make us glad for as many days as you have afflicted us, for as many years as we have seen trouble.
PSALM 90:14–15 NIV

For the Lord will not cast off forever, but, though he cause grief, he will have compassion according to the abundance of his steadfast love; for he does not afflict from his heart or grieve the children of men.
LAMENTATIONS 3:31–33 ESV

And we know that all things work together for good to them that love God, to them who are the called according to his purpose.
ROMANS 8:28 KJV

*He gives the barren woman a home, making her
the joyous mother of children. Praise the LORD!*
PSALM 113:9 ESV

*For You formed my inward parts; You covered me
in my mother's womb. I will praise You, for I am
fearfully and wonderfully made; marvelous are
Your works, and that my soul knows very well.*
PSALM 139:13–14 NKJV

*Now unto him that is able to do exceeding
abundantly above all that we ask or think,
according to the power that worketh in us,
unto him be glory in the church by Christ Jesus
throughout all ages, world without end. Amen.*
EPHESIANS 3:20–21 KJV

*Lord, I'm trying to accept whatever You want for my
life. But it's so hard. You know how much I long
for a child. Help me to give this longing to You.*

INJUSTICE

Did you know that in the Gospels, Jesus talks more about justice for those who are poor than He does about violence or sexual immorality? In fact, about a tenth of all the verses in the four Gospels have to do with concern for the poor.

We live in a world of injustice. This isn't fair. And God cares.

He wants us to care, too. He doesn't want us to look away from the world's injustice. He wants us to face it—and fight it.

Open your mouth for those who cannot speak, and for the rights of those who are left without help. Open your mouth. Be right and fair in what you decide. Stand up for the rights of those who are suffering and in need.
PROVERBS 31:8–9 NLV

"But if I were you, I would appeal to God; I would lay my cause before him. He performs wonders that cannot be fathomed, miracles that cannot be counted. . . . The lowly he sets on high, and those who mourn are lifted to safety. He thwarts the plans of the crafty, so that their hands achieve no success. . . . Darkness comes upon them in the daytime; at noon they grope as in the night. He saves the needy from the sword in their mouth; he saves them from the clutches of the powerful. So the poor have hope, and injustice shuts its mouth."

Job 5:8–9, 11–12, 14–16 NIV

The Lord within her is right and good. He will be fair and do nothing wrong. Every morning He brings to light what is fair. Every new day He is faithful. But the one who does wrong knows no shame.

Zephaniah 3:5 NLV

"Is not this the fast that I choose: to loose the bonds of wickedness, to undo the straps of the yoke, to let the oppressed go free, and to break every yoke?"

Isaiah 58:6 ESV

Moreover, I saw under the sun that in the place of justice, even there was wickedness, and in the place of righteousness, even there was wickedness. I said in my heart, God will judge the righteous and the wicked, for there is a time for every matter and for every work.
ECCLESIASTES 3:16–17 ESV

Joseph said to them, "Do not be afraid, for am I in the place of God? But as for you, you meant evil against me; but God meant it for good."
GENESIS 50:19–20 NKJV

Do not take revenge, my dear friends, but leave room for God's wrath, for it is written: "It is mine to avenge; I will repay," says the Lord.
ROMANS 12:19 NIV

Vindicate me, O God, and plead my cause against an ungodly nation; oh, deliver me from the deceitful and unjust man!
PSALM 43:1 NKJV

Do you not know that wrongdoers will not inherit
the kingdom of God? Do not be deceived.
1 CORINTHIANS 6:9 NIV

Your righteousness is like the mountains of God;
your judgments are like the great deep;
man and beast you save, O LORD.
PSALM 36:6 ESV

"But let what is fair roll down like waters. Let
what is right and good flow forever like a river."
AMOS 5:24 NLV

The LORD loves righteousness and justice;
the earth is full of his unfailing love.
PSALM 33:5 NIV

Do not lie against someone. And do not kill those
who are right and good or those who are not guilty.
For I will not free the guilty.
EXODUS 23:7 NLV

Blessed are they who observe justice,
who do righteousness at all times!
PSALM 106:3 ESV

It is a joy for the just to do justice, but destruction will come to the workers of iniquity.

PROVERBS 21:15 NKJV

Commit your way to the LORD; trust in him and he will do this: he will make your righteous reward shine like the dawn, your vindication like the noonday sun.

PSALM 37:5–6 NIV

For the LORD your God is God of gods and Lord of lords, the great, the mighty, and the awesome God, who is not partial and takes no bribe.

DEUTERONOMY 10:17 ESV

Behold my servant, whom I uphold, my chosen, in whom my soul delights; I have put my Spirit upon him; he will bring forth justice to the nations. He will not cry aloud or lift up his voice, or make it heard in the street; a bruised reed he will not break, and a faintly burning wick he will not quench; he will faithfully bring forth justice. He will not grow faint or be discouraged till he has established justice in the earth; and the coastlands wait for his law.

ISAIAH 42:1–4 ESV

Whoever sows injustice reaps calamity,
and the rod they wield in fury will be broken.
PROVERBS 22:8 NIV

When the world seems so unjust to me, Lord,
remind me that it treated You the same way.
Shift my focus away from myself. Show me ways to
help others whose situation is far worse than mine.

INSOMNIA

Insomnia makes us tired and cranky. When we're tired, we're more likely to feel anxious or depressed. It becomes a vicious cycle: The more upset and tense we become, the less we can sleep; the less we sleep, the more upset and tense we become. . . .

We may end up afraid to even go to bed because we don't want to face the frustration we feel when we lie there awake again. Anxiety overwhelms us. We feel helpless.

But God is with us, even when we lie awake night after night. He has compassion on our sleeplessness. His love never fails.

Take my yoke upon you, and learn of me;
for I am meek and lowly in heart:
and ye shall find rest unto your souls.
MATTHEW 11:29 KJV

Dear children, keep yourselves from idols.
1 JOHN 5:21 NIV

Truly my soul finds rest in God. . . .
Yes, my soul, find rest in God.
PSALM 62:1, 5 NIV

He gives His beloved sleep.
PSALM 127:2 NKJV

In peace I will both lie down and sleep;
for you alone, O LORD, make me dwell in safety.
PSALM 4:8 ESV

"Come to me, all you who are weary
and burdened, and I will give you rest."
MATTHEW 11:28 NIV

My God, I cry out by day, but you do not answer,
by night, but I find no rest. Yet you are enthroned
as the Holy One; you are the one Israel praises.
In you our ancestors put their trust; they trusted and
you delivered them. To you they cried out and were
saved; in you they trusted and were not put to shame.
PSALM 22:2–5 NIV

Sweet is the sleep of a laborer.
ECCLESIASTES 5:12 ESV

*Whoever dwells in the shelter of the Most High
will rest in the shadow of the Almighty.*
PSALM 91:1 NIV

*Return to your rest, O my soul.
For the Lord has been good to you.*
PSALM 116:7 NLV

*One day he got into a boat with his disciples, and
he said to them, "Let us go across to the other side
of the lake." So they set out, and as they sailed he
fell asleep. And a windstorm came down on the
lake, and they were filling with water and were
in danger. And they went and woke him, saying,
"Master, Master, we are perishing!" And he awoke
and rebuked the wind and the raging waves, and
they ceased, and there was a calm. He said to them,
"Where is your faith?"*
LUKE 8:22–25 ESV

*My people will abide in a peaceful habitation,
in secure dwellings, and in quiet resting places.*
ISAIAH 32:18 ESV

Surely I have calmed and quieted my soul,
like a weaned child with his mother;
like a weaned child is my soul within me.
PSALM 131:2 NKJV

Therefore I say unto you, What things soever ye
desire, when ye pray, believe that ye receive them,
and ye shall have them.
MARK 11:24 KJV

When I applied my mind to know wisdom and
to observe the labor that is done on earth—people
getting no sleep day or night—then I saw all that
God has done. No one can comprehend what goes
on under the sun. Despite all their efforts to search
it out, no one can discover its meaning. . . . So I
reflected on all this and concluded that the righteous
and the wise and what they do are in God's hands.
ECCLESIASTES 8:16–17; 9:1 NIV

You will keep him in perfect peace, whose mind
is stayed on You, because he trusts in You.
ISAIAH 26:3 NKJV

Do not worry. Learn to pray about everything.
Give thanks to God as you ask Him for what you
need. The peace of God is much greater than the
human mind can understand. This peace will keep
your hearts and minds through Christ Jesus.
PHILIPPIANS 4:6–7 NLV

I laid me down and slept; I awaked;
for the LORD sustained me.
PSALM 3:5 KJV

On my bed I remember You. I think of You through
the hours of the night. For You have been my help.
And I sing for joy in the shadow of Your wings. My
soul holds on to You. Your right hand holds me up.
PSALM 63:6–8 NLV

Dearest God, as I lie here in bed, may I feel the
echo of Your Spirit's breath in my own breathing.
May the peace of Your presence lie over me like a
blanket. May I recall all the things You have
done for me over the years. Help me to rest.

Prodigal Children

Few things hurt as much as watching our children go astray. We long to run after them and bring them home—and yet we must respect their decisions. We ache to protect them the way we did when they were small—but they have gone beyond our protection.

But even when our children were babies, they were never truly ours. They always belonged to God. Only He kept them safe. And none of that has changed. In the midst of what looks to us like chaos and confusion, He is there, leading our children into His peace.

All we like sheep have gone astray; we have turned every one to his own way; and the Lord has laid on [Christ] the iniquity of us all.
ISAIAH 53:6 ESV

You in Your mercy have led forth the people whom You have redeemed; You have guided them in Your strength to Your holy habitation.
EXODUS 15:13 NKJV

I am the good shepherd, and know my sheep, and am known of mine. As the Father knoweth me, even so know I the Father: and I lay down my life for the sheep. And other sheep I have, which are not of this fold: them also I must bring, and they shall hear my voice; and there shall be one fold, and one shepherd.
JOHN 10:14–16 KJV

*Rejoice always, pray without ceasing,
in everything give thanks; for this is
the will of God in Christ Jesus for you.*
1 THESSALONIANS 5:16–18 NKJV

*And we know that all things work together
for good to those who love God, to those
who are the called according to His purpose.*
ROMANS 8:28 NKJV

*"As a shepherd seeks out his flock on the day he is
among his scattered sheep, so will I seek out My
sheep and deliver them from all the places where
they were scattered on a cloudy and dark day."*
EZEKIEL 34:12 NKJV

"For my thoughts are not your thoughts, neither are your ways my ways," declares the LORD. "As the heavens are higher than the earth, so are my ways higher than your ways and my thoughts than your thoughts. As the rain and the snow come down from heaven, and do not return to it without watering the earth and making it bud and flourish, so that it yields seed for the sower and bread for the eater, so is my word that goes out from my mouth: It will not return to me empty, but will accomplish what I desire and achieve the purpose for which I sent it."

ISAIAH 55:8–11 NIV

The LORD has appeared of old to me, saying: "Yes, I have loved you with an everlasting love; therefore with lovingkindness I have drawn you."

JEREMIAH 31:3 NKJV

[Jesus] told them this parable: "What man of you, having a hundred sheep, if he has lost one of them, does not leave the ninety-nine in the open country, and go after the one that is lost. . . . Just so, I tell you, there will be more joy in heaven over one sinner who repents than over ninety-nine righteous persons who need no repentance."

LUKE 15:3–4, 7 ESV

Christian brothers, if a person is found doing some sin, you who are stronger Christians should lead that one back into the right way.
GALATIANS 6:1 NLV

The Lord is not slow to fulfill his promise as some count slowness, but is patient toward you, not wishing that any should perish, but that all should reach repentance.
2 PETER 3:9 ESV

"So [the prodigal] got up and went to his father. But while he was still a long way off, his father saw him and was filled with compassion for him; he ran to his son, threw his arms around him and kissed him."
LUKE 15:20 NIV

My heart feels broken, Father. I know You understand, for You, too, must be heartsick when You watch Your children choose paths that lead them toward brokenness and sorrow. Heal my children, I pray, Lord. Lead them in Your paths. I gave them to You when they were small—and now I give them to You again.

Sickness

No one enjoys being sick! But when sickness forces us to step back from life, to retreat to the small world of our beds, God is with us there. He will sustain us and restore us. He may even have something He wants to teach us during this time of illness!

When we face a chronic illness, we often feel a spectrum of emotions. All these feelings are normal. We will need help coping with this condition—doctors, counselors, friends, family—but most of all, we will need to find God even here, in the midst of our illness.

Beloved, I pray that all may go well with you and that you may be in good health, as it goes well with your soul.
3 John 1:2 esv

To every thing there is a season, and a time to every purpose under the heaven.
Ecclesiastes 3:1 kjv

Blessed be the God and Father of our Lord Jesus
Christ, the Father of mercies and God of all
comfort, who comforts us in all our affliction,
so that we may be able to comfort those who are
in any affliction, with the comfort with which we
ourselves are comforted by God.
2 CORINTHIANS 1:3–4 ESV

The LORD sustains them on their sickbed
and restores them from their bed of illness.
PSALM 41:3 NIV

The human spirit can endure in sickness.
PROVERBS 18:14 NIV

He gives strength to the weary and increases the
power of the weak. Even youths grow tired and
weary, and young men stumble and fall; but those
who hope in the LORD will renew their strength.
They will soar on wings like eagles; they will run and
not grow weary, they will walk and not be faint.
ISAIAH 40:29–31 NIV

For He will tell His angels to care for you
and keep you in all your ways. They will
hold you up in their hands.
PSALM 91:11–12 NLV

Pleasant words are as an honeycomb,
sweet to the soul, and health to the bones.
PROVERBS 16:24 KJV

Is anyone among you sick? Let him call for the
elders of the church, and let them pray over him,
anointing him with oil in the name of the Lord.
And the prayer of faith will save the sick,
and the Lord will raise him up.
JAMES 5:14–15 NKJV

"For I know the plans I have for you,"
says the Lord, "plans for well-being and not
for trouble, to give you a future and a hope."
JEREMIAH 29:11 NLV

"But for you who fear my name, the sun of
righteousness shall rise with healing in its wings."
MALACHI 4:2 ESV

And God shall wipe away all tears from their eyes;
and there shall be no more death, neither sorrow,
nor crying, neither shall there be any more pain:
for the former things are passed away.
REVELATION 21:4 KJV

But if the Spirit of Him who raised Jesus from
the dead dwells in you, He who raised Christ
from the dead will also give life to your mortal
bodies through His Spirit who dwells in you.
ROMANS 8:11 NKJV

Woe to me because of my injury! My wound
is incurable! Yet I said to myself, "This is
my sickness, and I must endure it."
JEREMIAH 10:19 NIV

For our light affliction, which is but for
a moment, is working for us a far more
exceeding and eternal weight of glory.
2 CORINTHIANS 4:17 NKJV

A cheerful heart is good medicine.
PROVERBS 17:22 NIV

He himself bore our sins in his body on the tree,
that we might die to sin and live to righteousness.
By his wounds you have been healed.
1 PETER 2:24 ESV

"Heal the sick in it [a town] and say to them,
'The kingdom of God has come near to you.'"
LUKE 10:9 ESV

He who lives in the safe place of the Most High will
be in the shadow of the All-powerful. I will say to
the Lord, "You are my safe and strong place, my
God, in Whom I trust." For it is He Who takes you
away from the trap, and from the killing sickness.
He will cover you with His wings. And under His
wings you will be safe. He is faithful like a
safe-covering and a strong wall.
PSALM 91:1–4 NLV

God, I know that every circumstance can lead us
to You, even sickness. I pray that You would use
this time of pain and illness for Your greater glory.

192

TOXIC FRIENDSHIPS

Often toxic friendships can creep up on us. We may not realize how unhealthy and poisonous a relationship has become until the problem is bigger than we know how to handle. Even once we recognize the problem, we may not know what to do.

God never wants us to be involved in something that isn't healthy for us, though. When we find ourselves involved in a toxic friendship, we need to ask Him to show us the way to freedom—for our sake, for the sake of our friend, and for His sake as well. He is not glorified by a relationship that damages and destroys!

"And if your right hand causes you to sin, cut it off and cast it from you; for it is more profitable for you that one of your members perish, than for your whole body to be cast into hell."
MATTHEW 5:30 NKJV

Happy is the man who does not walk in the way
sinful men tell him to, or stand in the path of
sinners, or sit with those who laugh at the truth.
But he finds joy in the Law of the Lord and thinks
about His Law day and night. This man is like
a tree planted by rivers of water, which gives its
fruit at the right time and its leaf never dries up.
Whatever he does will work out well for him.
PSALM 1:1–3 NLV

Do not be deceived: "Bad company
ruins good morals."
1 CORINTHIANS 15:33 ESV

A perverse person stirs up conflict,
and a gossip separates close friends.
PROVERBS 16:28 NIV

Do not make friends with a hot-tempered person,
do not associate with one easily angered, or you
may learn their ways and get yourself ensnared.
PROVERBS 22:24–25 NIV

My son, if sinners entice you, do not consent.
PROVERBS 1:10 NKJV

A friend loveth at all times,
and a brother is born for adversity.
PROVERBS 17:17 KJV

My children, let no one lead you in the wrong way.
The man who does what is right, is right with God
in the same way as Christ is right with God. The
person who keeps on sinning belongs to the devil.
The devil has sinned from the beginning. But the
Son of God came to destroy the works of the devil.
1 JOHN 3:7–8 NLV

Whoever walks with the wise becomes wise,
but the companion of fools will suffer harm.
PROVERBS 13:20 ESV

But avoid foolish controversies and genealogies
and arguments and quarrels about the law,
because these are unprofitable and useless.
Warn a divisive person once, and then warn
them a second time. After that, have nothing to
do with them. You may be sure that such people
are warped and sinful; they are self-condemned.
TITUS 3:9–11 NIV

Leave the presence of a fool, for there
you do not meet words of knowledge.
PROVERBS 14:7 ESV

Be ye not unequally yoked together with
unbelievers: for what fellowship hath
righteousness with unrighteousness?
and what communion hath light with darkness?
2 CORINTHIANS 6:14 KJV

Lord, give me wisdom to recognize when a friendship
is no longer healthy. I know that true friends support
one another. They accept one another. They reflect
Your love to one another. When I find myself involved
in a relationship that doesn't have these qualities,
give me the courage to make a change.

UNFORGIVENESS

It's not always easy to forgive. If we are Christ's followers, however, we must follow His example. If He could forgive the people who were killing Him, we can certainly find a way to forgive those who hurt us!

Ultimately, when we can't forgive, we hurt ourselves more than anyone. Nursing a grudge damages our own hearts. It can even make us physically ill.

God wants to set us free from old grievances and harbored resentments. He will heal our wounded hearts and give us the strength to forgive. After all, He forgave us!

Then Jesus said, "Father, forgive them, for they do not know what they do."
LUKE 23:34 NKJV

To the Lord our God belong mercies and forgiveness, though we have rebelled against him.
DANIEL 9:9 KJV

For if you forgive other people when they sin against you, your heavenly Father will also forgive you. But if you do not forgive others their sins, your Father will not forgive your sins.
MATTHEW 6:14–15 NIV

If you forgive a man, I forgive him also. If I have forgiven anything, I have done it because of you. Christ sees me as I forgive.
2 CORINTHIANS 2:10 NLV

Then Peter came up and said to him, "Lord, how often will my brother sin against me, and I forgive him? As many as seven times?" Jesus said to him, "I do not say to you seven times, but seventy-seven times."
MATTHEW 18:21–22 ESV

If anyone has caused grief, he has not so much grieved me as he has grieved all of you to some extent—not to put it too severely. The punishment inflicted on him by the majority is sufficient. Now instead, you ought to forgive and comfort him, so that he will not be overwhelmed by excessive sorrow. I urge you, therefore, to reaffirm your love for him.
2 CORINTHIANS 2:5–8 NIV

But I say unto you, That ye resist not evil:
but whosoever shall smite thee on thy
right cheek, turn to him the other also.
MATTHEW 5:39 KJV

The discretion of a man makes him slow to anger,
and his glory is to overlook a transgression.
PROVERBS 19:11 NKJV

You must be kind to each other. Think of the
other person. Forgive other people just as God
forgave you because of Christ's death on the cross.
EPHESIANS 4:32 NLV

We forgive so that Satan will not win.
We know how he works!
2 CORINTHIANS 2:11 NLV

Bear with each other and forgive one another
if any of you has a grievance against someone.
Forgive as the Lord forgave you.
COLOSSIANS 3:13 NIV

Wherefore I say unto thee, Her sins, which are
many, are forgiven; for she loved much: but to
whom little is forgiven, the same loveth little.
LUKE 7:47 KJV

"'And should not you have had mercy on your
fellow servant, as I had mercy on you?' And in
anger his master delivered him to the jailers,
until he should pay all his debt. So also my
heavenly Father will do to every one of you,
if you do not forgive your brother from your heart."
MATTHEW 18:33–35 ESV

"And whenever you stand praying, forgive,
if you have anything against anyone,
so that your Father also who is in heaven
may forgive you your trespasses."
MARK 11:25 ESV

"Judge not, and you shall not be judged.
Condemn not, and you shall not be condemned.
Forgive, and you will be forgiven."
LUKE 6:37 NKJV

Our Father which art in heaven, Hallowed be
thy name. Thy kingdom come. Thy will be done,
as in heaven, so in earth. Give us day by day our
daily bread. And forgive us our sins; for we also
forgive every one that is indebted to us.

"Pay attention to yourselves! If your brother sins,
rebuke him, and if he repents, forgive him,
and if he sins against you seven times in the day,
and turns to you seven times, saying,
'I repent,' you must forgive him."
LUKE 17:3–4 ESV

God, I know You want me to live at peace with others—
but I won't be able to do that until I can forgive.
Help me forgive that which seems unforgivable.
Free my heart so that I can be at peace with everyone.

201

VIOLENCE

Violence bombards us from all directions. It comes at us on the news, in movies, and on television. Violence touches our schools and our workplaces. It's evident at the global level—and it even comes into our homes.

We may think we have no part in this violence, but Jesus calls us to examine our hearts. He reminds us that if our thoughts are full of rage and hatred, then we, too, nurse the roots of violence inside our very beings. He asks us instead to become His hands and feet on this earth, spreading His peace.

Search me, O God, and know my heart: try me, and know my thoughts: and see if there be any wicked way in me, and lead me in the way everlasting.
PSALM 139:23–24 KJV

He shall redeem their soul from deceit and violence: and precious shall their blood be in his sight.
PSALM 72:14 KJV

"Peace I leave with you, My peace I give to you;
not as the world gives do I give to you. Let not
your heart be troubled, neither let it be afraid."
JOHN 14:27 NKJV

Violence shall no more be heard in thy land, wasting
nor destruction within thy borders; but thou shalt
call thy walls Salvation, and thy gates Praise.
ISAIAH 60:18 KJV

Bring to an end the violence of the wicked and
make the righteous secure—you, the righteous
God who probes minds and hearts.
PSALM 7:9 NIV

You will keep the man in perfect peace whose
mind is kept on You, because he trusts in You.
ISAIAH 26:3 NLV

For to us a child is born, to us a son is given,
and the government will be on his shoulders.
And he will be called Wonderful Counselor,
Mighty God, Everlasting Father, Prince of Peace.
ISAIAH 9:6 NIV

*And what shall I more say? for the time would fail
me to tell of Gedeon, and of Barak, and of Samson,
and of Jephthae; of David also, and Samuel, and of
the prophets: who through faith subdued kingdoms,
wrought righteousness, obtained promises, stopped
the mouths of lions, quenched the violence of fire,
escaped the edge of the sword, out of weakness were
made strong, waxed valiant in fight, turned to
flight the armies of the aliens.*
HEBREWS 11:32–34 KJV

*Let the peace of Christ rule in your hearts,
since as members of one body you were
called to peace. And be thankful.*
COLOSSIANS 3:15 NIV

*Whoever is pregnant with evil conceives trouble
and gives birth to disillusionment. Whoever digs
a hole and scoops it out falls into the pit they have
made. The trouble they cause recoils on them;
their violence comes down on their own heads.*
PSALM 7:14–16 NIV

Blessed are the meek, for they will inherit the earth.
MATTHEW 5:5 NIV

Lord, confuse the wicked, confound their words,
for I see violence and strife in the city.
PSALM 55:9 NIV

"You have heard that it was said, 'An eye for
an eye and a tooth for a tooth.' But I say to you,
Do not resist the one who is evil. But if anyone slaps
you on the right cheek, turn to him the other also."
MATTHEW 5:38–39 ESV

Dearly beloved, avenge not yourselves,
but rather give place unto wrath: for it is written,
Vengeance is mine; I will repay, saith the Lord.
ROMANS 12:19 KJV

Blessed are the peacemakers: for they
shall be called the children of God.
MATTHEW 5:9 KJV

These things I have spoken unto you, that in
me ye might have peace. In the world ye
shall have tribulation: but be of good cheer;
I have overcome the world.
JOHN 16:33 KJV

Finally, brothers, rejoice. Aim for restoration, comfort one another, agree with one another, live in peace; and the God of love and peace will be with you.
2 CORINTHIANS 13:11 ESV

"Lord, make me an instrument of Your peace. Where there is hatred, let me sow love. Where there is injury, pardon. Where there is doubt, faith. Where there is despair, hope. Where there is darkness, light. Where there is sadness, joy. O Divine Master, grant that I may not so much seek to be consoled as to console. To be understood as to understand, To be loved as to love. For it is in giving that we receive, it is in pardoning that we are pardoned," and it is in dying that we are born to eternal life.
—Prayer of Francis of Assisi

WEAKNESS

There are so many demands on our strength. So many crises to confront, so many problems to solve, so many people who need our help. We feel exhausted. We're not sure we can go on. Some days we'd like to just give up. We've reached the end of our strength.

But when we acknowledge our own weakness, that's the moment when the Holy Spirit can begin to work in our lives in new ways. When we throw up our own hands, God's hands have room to work.

But he said to me, "My grace is sufficient for you, for my power is made perfect in weakness." Therefore I will boast all the more gladly of my weaknesses, so that the power of Christ may rest upon me.
2 CORINTHIANS 12:9 ESV

I receive joy when I am weak. . . .
For when I am weak, then I am strong.
2 CORINTHIANS 12:10 NLV

But they that wait upon the LORD shall renew their strength; they shall mount up with wings as eagles; they shall run, and not be weary; and they shall walk, and not faint.
ISAIAH 40:31 KJV

Then Peter said, "Silver or gold I do not have, but what I do have I give you. In the name of Jesus Christ of Nazareth, walk." Taking him by the right hand, he helped him up, and instantly the man's feet and ankles became strong.
ACTS 3:6–7 NIV

But God chose what is foolish in the world to shame the wise; God chose what is weak in the world to shame the strong.
1 CORINTHIANS 1:27 ESV

I long to see you so that I may impart to you some spiritual gift to make you strong—that is, that you and I may be mutually encouraged by each other's faith.
ROMANS 1:11–12 NIV

And His name, through faith in His name,
has made this man strong, whom you see and know.
Yes, the faith which comes through Him has given
him this perfect soundness in the presence of you all.
ACTS 3:16 NKJV

I came to you in weakness with great fear
and trembling. My message and my preaching
were not with wise and persuasive words,
but with a demonstration of the Spirit's power,
so that your faith might not rest on human
wisdom, but on God's power.
1 CORINTHIANS 2:3–5 NIV

And what more shall I say? For the time
would fail me to tell of Gideon and Barak and
Samson and Jephthah, also of David and Samuel
and the prophets: who through faith subdued
kingdoms, worked righteousness, obtained promises,
stopped the mouths of lions, quenched the violence
of fire, escaped the edge of the sword, out of
weakness were made strong.
HEBREWS 11:32–34 NKJV

*For we do not have a High Priest who
cannot sympathize with our weaknesses.*
HEBREWS 4:15 NKJV

*The eye cannot say to the hand, "I don't need you!"
And the head cannot say to the feet, "I don't need
you!" On the contrary, those parts of the body
that seem to be weaker are indispensable.*
1 CORINTHIANS 12:21–22 NIV

Likewise the Spirit helps us in our weakness.
ROMANS 8:26 ESV

*"Everyone will be made cleaner
and stronger with fire."*
MARK 9:49 NLV

*So is it with the resurrection of the dead. What is
sown is perishable; what is raised is imperishable.
It is sown in dishonor; it is raised in glory.
It is sown in weakness; it is raised in power.*
1 CORINTHIANS 15:42–43 ESV

My body and my heart may grow weak, but God is the strength of my heart and all I need forever.
PSALM 73:26 NLV

For though He was crucified in weakness, yet He lives by the power of God. For we also are weak in Him, but we shall live with Him by the power of God toward you.
2 CORINTHIANS 13:4 NKJV

Watch, stand fast in the faith, be brave, be strong.
1 CORINTHIANS 16:13 NKJV

To the weak I became weak, to win the weak. I have become all things to all people so that by all possible means I might save some.
1 CORINTHIANS 9:22 NIV

Lord, You know how weak I am. But I can do all things through You. Heavenly Father, make me strong in You. May my strength come from Your might.

WORK

Our jobs are often the source of much of the
stress in our lives. Tight deadlines, multiple
responsibilities, conflicts with coworkers and
supervisors—all these can lead to tension.
We're likely to spend about half our lives in our
workplaces, though, so we need to find joy and
satisfaction, rather than stress and anxiety, in
our jobs.

We can learn to sense God's presence with
us as we work. Even on our busiest days, we
need to take time to whisper a prayer or spend a
quiet moment with our Lord.

*By the seventh day God had finished the work he
had been doing; so on the seventh day he rested
from all his work. Then God blessed the seventh
day and made it holy, because on it he rested from
all the work of creating that he had done.*
GENESIS 2:2–3 NIV

He who works with a lazy hand is poor, but the hand of the hard worker brings riches. A son who gathers in summer is wise, but a son who sleeps during gathering time brings shame.

PROVERBS 10:4–5 NLV

Therefore, I urge you, brothers and sisters, in view of God's mercy, to offer your bodies as a living sacrifice, holy and pleasing to God—this is your true and proper worship. Do not conform to the pattern of this world, but be transformed by the renewing of your mind. Then you will be able to test and approve what God's will is—his good, pleasing and perfect will.

ROMANS 12:1–2 NIV

The people of Israel were sad in their spirit because of being servants. They cried for help. And because of their hard work their cry went up to God. God heard their crying and remembered His agreement with Abraham, Isaac and Jacob. God saw the people of Israel and He cared about them.

EXODUS 2:23–25 NLV

*When you eat the labor of your hands, you shall
be happy, and it shall be well with you.*
PSALM 128:2 NKJV

*"Do not work for the food that perishes, but for
the food that endures to eternal life, which the
Son of Man will give to you. For on him
God the Father has set his seal."*
JOHN 6:27 ESV

*Whatever you do, work at it with all your heart,
as working for the Lord, not for human masters,
since you know that you will receive an inheritance
from the Lord as a reward. It is the Lord Christ
you are serving.*
COLOSSIANS 3:23–24 NIV

Some good comes from all work.
PROVERBS 14:23 NLV

*And I heard a voice from heaven saying, "Write this:
Blessed are the dead who die in the Lord from now
on." "Blessed indeed," says the Spirit, "that they may
rest from their labors, for their deeds follow them!"*
REVELATION 14:13 ESV

But we urge you, brethren, that you increase more and more; that you also aspire to lead a quiet life, to mind your own business, and to work with your own hands, as we commanded you, that you may walk properly toward those who are outside, and that you may lack nothing.

1 Thessalonians 4:10–12 nkjv

Do not be lazy but always work hard. Work for the Lord with a heart full of love for Him.

Romans 12:11 nlv

I glorified you on earth, having accomplished the work that you gave me to do.

John 17:4 esv

If a man works, his pay is not a gift. It is something he has earned.

Romans 4:4 nlv

Yes, God kept us from what looked like sure death and He is keeping us. As we trust Him, He will keep us in the future.

2 Corinthians 1:10 nlv

*Consider the lilies of the field, how they grow; they
toil not, neither do they spin: and yet I say unto you,
That even Solomon in all his glory was not arrayed
like one of these. Wherefore, if God so clothe the grass
of the field, which to day is, and to morrow is cast
into the oven, shall he not much more clothe you,
O ye of little faith?*
MATTHEW 6:28–30 KJV

*"Come to Me, all you who labor and are heavy
laden, and I will give you rest. Take My yoke upon
you and learn from Me, for I am gentle and lowly
in heart, and you will find rest for your souls.
For My yoke is easy and My burden is light."*
MATTHEW 11:28–30 NKJV

*Heavenly Lord, thank You for my job. May I be
challenged and inspired by the work I do. Even in the
midst of stress, even on the days when I fail, may I look
away from my own feelings and see You—and beyond
You, a world that needs my efforts, no matter how small
they may seem. Give me the will and strength to work
hard today. May I find gladness in my efforts,
and most of all, may I please You.*

WORRY

Guess what the Old German root word of *worry* means. It means "to strangle"! Worries strangle us. They hinder our ability to breathe in the Spirit of God. Worries interfere with the flow of God's life into ours.

But our worries can be turned into prayers. Each time a worry occurs to us, we need to form the habit of lifting it up to God. As we offer our worries to Him, they will lose their stranglehold on our lives. And then we will find ourselves instead thanking God for all He has done.

Do not worry. Learn to pray about everything. Give thanks to God as you ask Him for what you need.
PHILIPPIANS 4:6 NLV

"Therefore I tell you, do not worry about your life, what you will eat or drink; or about your body, what you will wear. Is not life more than food, and the body more than clothes?"
MATTHEW 6:25 NIV

"Do not worry about the things that belong to you.
For the best of all the land of Egypt is yours."
GENESIS 45:20 NLV

"Can any one of you by worrying
add a single hour to your life?"
MATTHEW 6:27 NIV

My soul also is greatly troubled; but You, O LORD—
how long? Return, O LORD, deliver me!
PSALM 6:3–4 NKJV

Do not worry yourself because of those who
do wrong, and do not be jealous of the sinful.
For there will be no future for the sinful man.
The lamp of the sinful will be put out.
PROVERBS 24:19–20 NLV

"But when they deliver you up, do not worry
about how or what you should speak. For it will be
given to you in that hour what you should speak."
MATTHEW 10:19 NKJV

"The seed that fell among thorns stands for those who hear, but as they go on their way they are choked by life's worries, riches and pleasures, and they do not mature. But the seed on good soil stands for those with a noble and good heart, who hear the word, retain it, and by persevering produce a crop."

LUKE 8:14–15 NIV

"But blessed is the one who trusts in the LORD, whose confidence is in him. They will be like a tree planted by the water that sends out its roots by the stream. It does not fear when heat comes; its leaves are always green. It has no worries in a year of drought and never fails to bear fruit."

JEREMIAH 17:7–8 NIV

And Jesus answered and said unto her, Martha, Martha, thou art careful and troubled about many things: but one thing is needful: and Mary hath chosen that good part, which shall not be taken away from her.

LUKE 10:41–42 KJV

Give all your worries to Him
because He cares for you.
1 PETER 5:7 NLV

Do not fret because of those who are evil. . . . Trust
in the LORD and do good; dwell in the land and
enjoy safe pasture. Take delight in the LORD, and he
will give you the desires of your heart. Commit your
way to the LORD; trust in him and he will do this:
He will make your righteous reward shine like the
dawn, your vindication like the noonday sun.
Be still before the LORD and wait patiently for him;
do not fret when people succeed in their ways,
when they carry out their wicked schemes.
PSALM 37:1, 3–7 NIV

When my worry is great within me,
Your comfort brings joy to my soul.
PSALM 94:19 NLV

"Therefore do not worry about tomorrow, for
tomorrow will worry about its own things.
Sufficient for the day is its own trouble."
MATTHEW 6:34 NKJV

Let not your heart be troubled: ye believe in God, believe also in me. In my Father's house are many mansions: if it were not so, I would have told you. I go to prepare a place for you. And if I go and prepare a place for you, I will come again, and receive you unto myself; that where I am, there ye may be also.
JOHN 14:1–3 KJV

Thank You, Father, for giving me the confidence that You are for me and with me. I know that life holds nothing that You can't overcome. No power is greater than You. I can rest in Your arms today, knowing that You have everything under control.